GET
CODING 2!

WRITTEN BY DAVID WHITNEY

ILLUSTRATED BY DUNCAN BEEDIE

CANDLEWICK PRESS

CONTENTS

ABOUT THIS BOOK

Welcome to *Get Coding 2!*, where you're going to learn all about games and gaming. In this book, you will explore the fascinating history of computer games and learn about some of the most famous and popular games that are played all over the world. Best of all, you'll discover how to code your own games, from simple turn-based games like *Noughts and Crosses* (tic-tac-toe) to more complicated games with graphics.

Are you ready for some exciting coding missions?

what does this book teach you?

We all know how important computers are and that they can do incredible things. You can play games that are so realistic, you feel like you are right there in the world of the game. But computers can't do things by themselves. When you play your favorite computer game and there are sneaky enemies, complicated graphics, and atmospheric music, it's because someone has written a set of instructions for your computer to follow so it can create all the different elements. These instructions are known as a program, and they have to be written in a language, or code, that the computer can understand.

This book is going to teach you how to code web-based computer games using the programming languages HTML and JavaScript. HTML and JavaScript are two of the most popular languages in the world. You might not have written programs using these languages before, but every time you use the Internet, whether it is to check a website or play a game, you will be using programs created in them. HTML builds the basic structure of a web page, and JavaScript makes the page interactive so it responds to the user. Using these two languages, you can create games that will challenge the player and give endless hours of fun.

Go to
www.getcodingkids.com
for help and support

How does this book work?

There are five chapters in this book. In each chapter, there is a top-secret mission that teaches you how to code a different game. Using JavaScript, you will build different types of games, make your game respond to the player, discover how to code simple graphics, create animations, and even add artificial intelligence (AI) to your game. In each mission, you will be joining the Lucky Cat Club: Ruby, Markus, Grace, Rusty, and Scratch. They need your help to defeat SaberTooth Studios, their gaming rivals.

What do you need?

All you need is access to a computer (PC or Mac) that is connected to the Internet. It might be helpful if you have written programs in HTML and JavaScript before, but don't worry if you haven't, since we'll cover all the basics. And if you get stuck, you can go to our website for help and support: **www.getcodingkids.com**.

Markus   Grace   Rusty   Ruby

Are you ready to get coding?

scratch

We hope you enjoy this book and that it inspires you to get coding!

INTRODUCTION
COMPUTER GAMES

Every day we use computers of different shapes and sizes to do a huge range of things. Computers are made up of hardware (the things you can touch such as the keyboard and screen) and software (the things you can't touch but that a computer needs to work). An important type of software is the program: a detailed set of instructions that the computer follows in order to complete a task. Programs are written in code, and writing programs is known as coding. Games are special kinds of programs that run on your computer, but instead of letting you browse the Internet or do your homework, they let you play and have fun.

If you have access to a computer, phone, tablet, or games console, you've probably played a game. They're everywhere! *Pokémon GO*, *Super Mario Bros.*, *Minecraft,* and *Angry Birds* are all popular computer games. But what is the secret to making a great game?

Why do we play?

People play games for all different reasons: some love the challenge of beating a score or obstacle; others enjoy competing with other players or the thrill of exploring new worlds and experiences. Games can be about anything—from made-up characters and universes to football games or puzzles. They often fall into categories, which game designers call genres.

Who do we play with?

Games can involve a single player playing against a computer. They can also be played over the Internet, which means you and someone thousands of miles away could be working together to defeat the same enemy. When you play against a computer—whether the computer acts as the second player in a game of chess or the enemy that has to be defeated at the end of a level—the computer isn't thinking and acting by itself. It has been programmed to have artificial intelligence (AI), so it responds in the same way a player would. But no matter what the game's genre or how many players are involved, there are certain things that all games have in common.

what makes a great game?

A great game makes you want to play it again and again. Game designers spend hours putting the different elements of a game together to give the player the best experience possible. A game needs a good character or story and a world that you believe in. Interesting **graphics** and sounds are often used to create an atmosphere. The game needs to be fun to play, but it must also contain the right level of challenge. Often a game will start off easily and then get more difficult.

One thing that all games have in common are rules that tell the player what they can and can't do. Good games have rules that surprise the player or are difficult to win against. A game also needs to have a clear goal. Does the player have to solve a puzzle, defeat an enemy, or collect objects? Often there will be a mixture of small goals, such as collecting an object, and big goals, such as defeating an enemy at the end of a level. The game needs to be designed in a way that gives the player feedback if they achieve or fail to achieve their goal. They might score points, beat the clock, or progress to the next level. Or they might lose points or lives.

A great game has the perfect balance of all these different elements.

CODE WORDS

GRAPHICS are the things you see on your computer screen that aren't text. Graphics can be photos, illustrations, diagrams, or images.

Game Genres

o **Action:** a fast-paced game in which the player gets caught up in the drama, often having to survive against different enemies or threats

o **Combat:** a game in which the player has to defeat one or several opponents

o **Platformer:** a game in which the player has to run and jump from platform to platform in levels of increasing complexity

o **Puzzle:** a game that involves solving a problem, often under time pressure

o **Role-playing:** a game in which the player becomes a character, normally in a fantasy world; the game often involves a magical storyline and the player completing a quest

o **Sandbox:** a game in which the player can explore the world at their own speed and create their own adventures

o **Simulation:** a game in which the world or characters are similar to real life

o **Sport:** a game in which the player plays a sport such as football or drives a racecar

o **Strategy:** a game that makes the player think and make choices; the player will often have to make decisions that affect the whole world and many characters

Let's take a look at the history of gaming.

A BRIEF HISTORY OF GAMING

We love to play, and for thousands of years, people have been inventing games. You've probably played a board game such as Scrabble, Monopoly, or Clue. But did you know that some board games date back thousands of years to ancient Egypt?

Computer games are a much more recent invention, but they have lots in common with simple board games. In fact, the first computer games were so basic that you probably wouldn't recognize them compared to today's games with their sophisticated graphics, music, and multiplayer capabilities.

1950s: The first computer games

For as long as we've had computers, people have wanted to play with them.

In the 1950s, computers were room-size pieces of machinery that you couldn't interact with much. But a mathematician named A. S. Douglas managed to develop a rudimentary computer tic-tac-toe game called *OXO*. The game's grid and progress were displayed on a small, primitive screen. In 1958, physicist William Higinbotham created a slightly more sophisticated game called *Tennis for Two*, in which each player used a control knob and a button to hit the ball over the net.

In 1961, computer scientists at the Massachusetts Institute of Technology inaugurated hacker culture by exploring what their new computer, the DEC PDP-1, could do. Although it still didn't look much like today's computers, the PDP-1 had a screen and typewriter and was programmable. Of course one of the many programs the MIT crew developed was a game.

1960s: *Spacewar!*

The first computer game for this PDP-1 at MIT was written in 1962 by three developers: Martin Graetz, Steve Russell, and Wayne Wiitanen. They called the game *Spacewar!*

It was a two-player game, with each player controlling a spaceship. The aim of the game was to shoot at the other ship. The game was immediately popular and shared with other universities for them to test on their new PDP-1 computers.

At the time *Spacewar!* was written, the few computers that existed all had their own programming languages, which meant that a game written for one computer probably would not run on another. During the 1960s, lots of small games were written for the big expensive computers in universities and schools because of how much fun everyone had with *Spacewar!*

In the 1960s, programming languages that ran on more than one computer, such as BASIC, were invented. This meant that games could be shared more widely and as a result became increasingly popular.

1970s: Early games and arcades

In the 1970s, Nolan Bushnell started a company called Atari to make games that could be played in amusement arcades and theme parks. Their second product, a table tennis game called *Pong*, was a huge hit and started the computer game industry, which is now worth billions of dollars. These early games were made from electronic circuits and didn't even use code to run.

At the same time, a company called Magnavox released its first game **console**, a home computer that plugged into a TV, which had its own version of a table tennis game included.

CODE WORDS A game **CONSOLE** (also known as a home console) is a small computer that connects to a television or monitor for playing computer games.

Did you know?

Early home computers let you create games by typing in code. You could buy magazines full of code for different games. All you had to do was type it into your computer to run the game.

Games have changed so much throughout history!

1980s: Consoles

By the early 1980s, Nolan Bushnell's dreams had come true. Arcades were everywhere and full of 2-D games that are now regarded as classics, including *Pac-Man*, *Missile Command*, and *Donkey Kong*—the first game to feature the character Mario. During this period, Atari and Commodore continued to launch new consoles. The first consoles from Nintendo and Sega were also released.

In 1984, the IBM PC/AT and the Apple Macintosh, the two computers that are most like the ones we use today, went on sale. Games for these new computers were launched as well.

1990s: Going 3-D

Games in the 1990s became faster, more colorful and complicated, and featured iconic characters such as Sonic the Hedgehog and Mario. Sports games started to become popular, with the first version of *FIFA* released in 1993. In the late 1990s, 3-D graphics took over with games like *Doom* on the IBM PC and *Super Mario 64* on the Nintendo 64.

2000s: Blockbusters

Through the 2000s, games became as popular as films—and began to make more money than blockbusters. Sony developed the PlayStation and introduced characters such as Crash Bandicoot and games that are still popular today, including *Final Fantasy*, *Metal Gear Solid*, and *Gran Turismo*.

Microsoft joined the gaming industry, releasing their Xbox console in 2001 with bestsellers such as *Halo* and *Fable*. Game series from the 1990s, such as *Super Mario* and *The Legend of Zelda*, reinvented themselves to stay fresh.

Gaming today

In the late 2000s and early 2010s, games continued to evolve, with gamers fighting dragons in massive multiplayer games such as *World of Warcraft* and unleashing their inner rock star in *Guitar Hero*. The Nintendo Wii, released in 2006, brought games to people who previously didn't think computer games were for them.

From 2008, there was an explosion in cell-phone games. Some of the most popular are puzzle games like *Angry Birds*, endless runner games like *Canabalt*, and addictive matching games like *Candy Crush Saga*. As phones developed into tablets, the same games could be played on them too.

Today, companies such as Atari and Commodore no longer exist, but many games and characters are still the same. Mario has appeared in over 200 games since 1981 with more than 240 million copies sold worldwide.

Famous games

- *Doom*
- *FIFA*
- *Fortnite*
- *GoldenEye 007*
- *Halo*
- *Mario series*
- *Minecraft*
- *Pac-Man*
- *Rock Band*
- *Sonic the Hedgehog*
- *World of Warcraft*
- *The Legend of Zelda*

Famous characters

- Angry Birds
- Crash Bandicoot
- Donkey Kong
- Lara Croft
- Master Chief
- Mario
- Pac-Man
- Sonic

GREAT GAMES AND COOL CONSOLES

OXO by A. S. Douglas (1952)

Pong by Atari (1972)

Donkey Kong by Nintendo (1981)

Commodore 64 released (1982)

Nintendo Game Boy released (1989)

Sega Genesis released (1988)

Nintendo NES released (1983)

IBM PC/AT and Apple Macintosh released (1984)

Sony PlayStation released (1994)

Nintendo 64 released (1996)

Snake by Nokia (1998)

Sega Dreamcast released (1998)

Sony PlayStation 3 and Nintendo Wii released (2006)

Microsoft Xbox 360 released (2005)

Microsoft Xbox released (2001)

Sony PlayStation 2 released (2000)

Apple iPhone released (2007) Apple iPad released (2010)

Canabalt by Semi-Secret Software (2009)

Sony PlayStation 4 and Microsoft Xbox One released (2013)

I love my console!

Nintendo Switch released (2017)

HOW TO CODE A GAME

Did you know that even though games have become bigger and more complicated, the way we make them is still the same as in the 1980s? Games are built by teams of people. The game designers work out what should be in a game to make it fun. Game programmers and artists then take their designs and write programs and create graphics to bring the game to life.

Like all programs, games can be written in lots of different languages, but some of the most commonly used languages to write games are C, C++, C#, and JavaScript. We're going to learn how to write games using JavaScript. This means that the game will run in a web browser.

Let's learn how to write games using JavaScript!

JavaScript

JavaScript is one of the most popular programming languages in the world. It runs on lots of different types of computers, including right inside your web browser, the program that you use to access the Internet. You can use JavaScript with other programming languages such as HTML and CSS to create all kinds of web programs, apps, and games. A programming language is built from special keywords that the computer understands, along with a set of rules about how you write the code. We call the keywords and these rules the syntax of a programming language.

How to Write JavaScript

JavaScript syntax looks complicated since it is made up of a mixture of words and symbols. All you are really doing, though, is storing information, or data, so your computer can use it to do the things you want it to do. In JavaScript, we use variables to store data. You define a variable by using the variable keyword and then giving the variable a name. Then you use the assignment operator (=) to give your variable a value. Variables store three types of values: strings, numbers, and Booleans (a type that has two values—usually true or false):

variable name

variable keyword

```
var aString = "A string is a set of words";
var aNumber = 123;
var aBoolean = true;
```

variable value

assignment operator

We use variables with operators such as equal to (==), addition (+), and less than (<) and with statements such as the if statement to make a program that can perform actions. We can also use built-in functions to do things in the browser, such as pop up alerts. Look at this example:

variable

if statement

```
var javascriptIsFun = true;
var message = "JavaScript is fun!";
if(javascriptIsFun) {
        alert(message);
}
```

built-in alert function

> Run this code and an alert will pop up in your browser. Find out how to do this in the next section.

JavaScript

X

JavaScript is fun!

OK

13

HOW TO USE THIS BOOK

The Lucky Cat Club needs your help! Ruby, Markus, Grace, and Rusty have to learn how to code five different games so they'll be ready for the Game On Hackathon. They need to beat their rivals SaberTooth Studios and show them that gaming is for everyone. Your job is to work through each mission and master all the different coding skills needed to build the games.

Mission Briefs

At the start of each chapter, you will receive a Mission Brief from a Lucky Cat Club member that will tell you all about the game they want to code. Keep an eye out for the new skills you are going to learn to code *Tic-Tac-Toe, Snake, Table Tennis,* and much more.

Game Builds

The code for each of the games has been broken down into bite-size chunks. Follow the step-by-step instructions in each Game Build to create your game. And don't worry if you get stuck because you can always go to the *Get Coding!* website (**www.getcodingkids.com**), where you can find every piece of code in this book.

Games

By the end of each mission, you will have built a game of your own and picked up lots of new skills on the way. Have fun playing the game and then go to the *Get Coding!* website to find ideas for how to develop it further.

The Developer's Dictionary

The Lucky Cat Club's favorite website is the Developer's Dictionary. Learn about the history of games and gaming and use this information to help you complete the missions.

KEY CODE SKILLS

Before you receive the brief for Mission 1, there are some basic Code Skills you need to learn. You will use these skills throughout the entire book, so it's important to get a handle on them now. You can code using a PC or a Mac, but you have to create and save your HTML file in a different way depending on which system you are using.

KEY CODE SKILL 1 ▶ **CREATING A FOLDER**

You need to have a place in your computer where you can save all your HTML files. Make a folder on your desktop called **Coding 2**. It's really important that you save all your HTML files in the same place, so make sure you keep using this folder as you work through the missions.

PC	On a PC, right-click on your desktop and click *New* and then *Folder*. Call your new folder **Coding 2**.
Mac	On a Mac, hold down the Control key and click on your desktop. Then select *New Folder*. Call your new folder **Coding 2**.

Master these essential Code Skills and you'll be ready for the first mission!

KEY CODE SKILL 2 ► CREATING AN HTML FILE

You need to know how to create an HTML file so you can write code. Programmers normally use specialist software to write code (see page 221 for details), but all computers come with text-editing programs that let you write HTML files. If you have a PC, you can use Notepad. If you have a Mac, you can use TextEdit.

PC

On a PC, you'll find Notepad by going into the *Start* menu and typing it in the search bar.

Mac

On a Mac, you'll find TextEdit by typing it in the *Spotlight* search magnifying glass in the top right of your screen. When you open TextEdit, you need to do the following things:
- Set up your file as a plain text (rather than rich text) file. To do this, go to *Format* in the menu bar and select *Make Plain Text*.
- Also go to *TextEdit* in the menu bar. Select *Preferences*. In the *New Document* tab in the *Format* section, make sure *Plain text* is checked. In the *Options* section, make sure *Smart quotes* is unchecked.
- In the *Open and Save* tab in *Preferences,* make sure *Display HTML files as HTML code instead of formatted text* is checked.

KEY CODE SKILL 3 ► SAVING YOUR HTML FILE

When you save your HTML file, you need to make sure you save it using the file extension **.html** at the end of your file name. Your computer uses file extensions to work out how to open files. By giving your file the extension **.html**, you're telling your computer that it should open the file in a web browser.

PC

On a PC, you need to:
- Go to *File* and select *Save As.*
- Select the **Coding 2** folder as the destination to save the file to.
- Choose a name for your file, such as Mission 1, and type it into the *File name* bar.
- After the name of the file, type **.html** so your file name reads **Mission1.html**. Click *Save.*

Mac

On a Mac, you need to:
- Go to *File* and select *Save.*
- Select your **Coding 2** folder as the destination to save your file to.
- Choose a name for your file, such as Mission 1, and type it into the *Save As* bar.
- After the name of the file, type **.html** so your file name reads **Mission1.html**.
- Make sure the check box *If no extension is provided, use ".txt"* is unchecked. Click *Save.*

KEY CODE SKILL 4 ► OPENING YOUR HTML FILE

To see your code displayed on-screen, you need to open your HTML file in a web browser. You then might want to go back into your text-editing program to make some changes to your code.

PC

On a PC, you need to:
- Save your file, as described in Key Code Skill 3.
- Open your **Coding 2** folder on your desktop. Double-click on your HTML file. It will open in your web browser.
- When you want to edit your code, right-click on the HTML file in your **Coding 2** folder. Select *Open with* and choose Notepad.

Mac

On a Mac, you need to:
- Save your file, as described in Key Code Skill 3.
- Open your **Coding 2** folder on your desktop. Double-click on your HTML file. It will open in your web browser.
- When you want to edit your code, right-click on the HTML file in your **Coding 2** folder. Select *Open with* and choose TextEdit.

KEY CODE SKILL 5 ► USING DEVELOPER TOOLS

As you code the Game Builds and open your code in the browser, you may find that the code isn't displaying in the way you expected. Don't worry! You can use the developer tools that are built into your browser to help you find the bug. You'll find the developer tools in your browser settings. On a PC, try the keyboard shortcut *F12*. On a Mac, try the shortcut *Command + Option + I*. Or right-click on the page and select *Inspect*. Go to the elements tools in the console and look for where the errors are occurring.

KEY CODE SKILL 6 ► USING THE *GET CODING!* WEBSITE

Don't forget that as you work through the book, you can use the *Get Coding!* website to help you with your missions. If you get stuck at any point when you're writing code, go to the website and see what your code block should look like. You can even copy and paste the code blocks from the website into your text-editing program. You will find all the files you need for Mission 5 on the website.

The *Get Coding!* URL is **www.getcodingkids.com**.

Mission 1

NOUGHTS AND CROSSES

- LEARN TO USE JAVASCRIPT WITH HTML

- BUILD AN INTERACTIVE GAME BOARD

- CREATE A TURN-BASED GAME STATE WITH TWO PLAYERS

- CODE A LOOP TO CHECK FOR A WINNER

- FIX BUGS AND SIMPLIFY YOUR CODE

Mission Brief

To	me@getcoding.com
Cc	Markus; Grace; Rusty; Scratch
Subject	Mission 1 brief

Hello,

It's great to meet you. My name is Ruby Day and I'm a scientist. I'm a world expert on dinosaur fossils, which is a pretty fun job (apart from when you get stuck in freezing Siberia with a nutty professor and a stolen diamond — but that's another story).

When I'm not away on expeditions or in the lab looking at pieces of rock that are millions of years old, I love computer games. I like the challenges and the characters, and I love trying to win! And games are so fun to play. At the moment, my favorite games are puzzles. My best friends, Rusty, Grace, and Markus, are all gamers too, and between us, we play every kind of game, from sports games to endless runners.

We've now decided that we're not just going to play games but also try coding them. We're calling ourselves the Lucky Cat Club, after my cat, Scratch, who is going to be our mascot. Our plan is to learn to code five different games so we can compete in the Game On Hackathon at the end of the month. We'll have to show our games to a panel of judges. Exciting!

We'd love you to help us with the coding so we can build the games in time for the hackathon. Another group, called SaberTooth Studios, is going to be there, and they're really famous and great coders. Have you heard of *Tiger Trail*? That's the adventure game they built. They've been posting online about the hackathon, saying new gamers shouldn't bother going since they're the best team and are going to win. We want to show them that the Lucky Cat Club can code too, and beat them to the trophy.

Will you join our team and help us? The first game we're going to code is *Noughts and Crosses*. I hope it's not too much of a puzzle!

Purr-fect wishes,

Ruby

Noughts and Crosses

From the Developer's Dictionary: Your Guide to Games and Gaming

This entry is about Noughts and Crosses. For other turn-based games, see Turn-Based Strategy Games.

Noughts and Crosses (also known as tic-tac-toe) is one of the oldest games in the world. In the game, two players take turns to put either an O (nought) or an X (cross) into a <u>grid</u> that measures 3 x 3 (three columns across and three rows high). One player places only X's in the boxes, and the other places only O's.

Noughts and Crosses

Genre:	Turn-based game
Mode:	Two-player
First release:	1952 (as OXO)
Playing time:	Less than 1 minute
Skills required:	Strategy, tactics, and observation

To win the game, a player has to place either three X's or three O's in a line, horizontally (across), vertically (up and down), or diagonally. The other player must try to stop them. The first person to get three in a row wins.

Noughts and Crosses is a turn-based game, which means that the players take turns. When it's a player's turn, that player is in control of what happens in the game, while the other player must wait until it is their turn. Turn-based games are very common, and many board games, such as chess, work in this way. They are popular because players must use strategy to win.

The first Noughts and Crosses game on a computer, called _OXO_, was created in 1952, making it one of the earliest computer games. The user played against the computer rather than another person, making it one of the earliest examples of artificial intelligence. The computer was able to react to what the player did without the player knowing what decision it would make. Originally _OXO_ used small lights known as LEDs to display the game board.

NOUGHTS AND CROSSES

Instead of playing Noughts and Crosses using a paper and pen, we are going to learn how to code the game so you can play it in your web browser against a friend. We are going to use three programming languages: HTML, CSS, and JavaScript. HTML will form the basic structure of the game, CSS will allow us to design it, and JavaScript will make the game interactive.

To make things simple, the game has been broken down into small sections. Work through the mission and discover the skills that you need for the game. Then complete the Game Builds by following the step-by-step instructions. By the end of the mission, you will have built your own version of *Noughts and Crosses*. Are you ready to play?

> Don't forget to use the *Get Coding!* website if you get stuck.

The Game Build

We want our game board to be three columns across and three rows high. Two players will play against each other. Each player will take turns clicking a box, and either an X or an O will be displayed. We need code that can keep track of which player's turn it is and whether a player has won. We also need to code an alert so that when a player wins, a box pops up and the game ends. Remember that there are three ways to form a winning lineup: vertically, horizontally, and diagonally.

O wins vertically

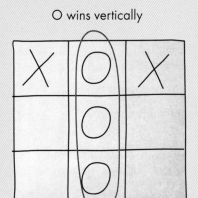

X wins horizontally

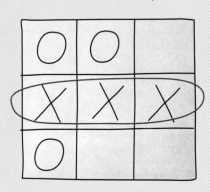

O wins diagonally

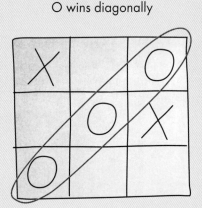

At the end of the mission, your finished game will look like this:

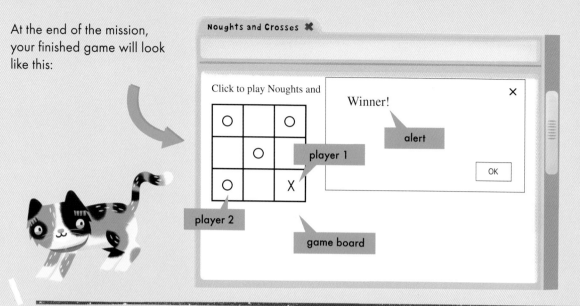

THE GAME BOARD

The first thing we are going to code is the game board. To do this, we need to use HTML and CSS. HTML is a programming language made up of elements, which are created using small pieces of code called tags. Each tag gives your web browser an instruction for how to display the information. You put the information between an opening tag and a closing tag. Here's a very simple HTML web page:

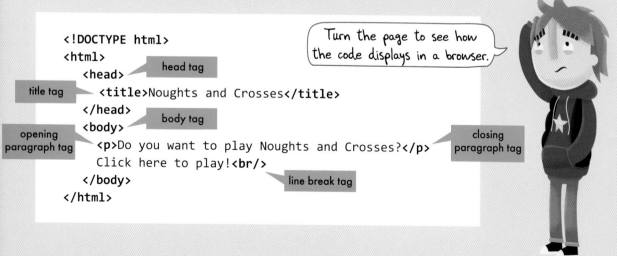

```
<!DOCTYPE html>
<html>
    <head>                          head tag
title tag     <title>Noughts and Crosses</title>
    </head>
    <body>                          body tag
opening
paragraph tag   <p>Do you want to play Noughts and Crosses?</p>   closing
                Click here to play!<br/>                           paragraph tag
    </body>                         line break tag
</html>
```

Turn the page to see how the code displays in a browser.

The information inside the `<head>` tag is not displayed in the body of the page. This is where you have the title of the web page and give your browser instructions to apply to the whole page, rather than individual elements.

Inside the `<body>` tag is the information we see displayed on-screen. Here we have used the paragraph `<p>` and line break `<br/>` to format the text:

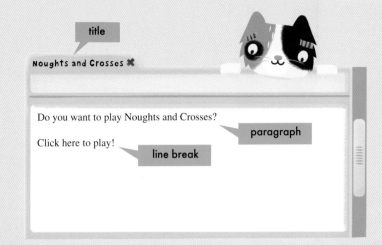

title

Noughts and Crosses ✖

Do you want to play Noughts and Crosses?

Click here to play!

paragraph

line break

The `<div>` Tag

Our game board needs to be three columns across and three rows high. To create the structure of the board, we need to use the HTML `<div>` tag. It looks like this:

```
<body>
    <div>
        <p>Ruby</p>
        <p>Scratch</p>
    </div>
</body>
```

`<div>` tag

elements inside `<div>`

DIV ✖

Ruby

Scratch

The `<div>` tag is a bit like an invisible box: it allows you to group lots of HTML elements. The `<div>` tag makes designing a web page easier because it means you can easily apply formatting to all the elements inside the `<div>` tag rather than having to format each individual HTML element.

24

Using CSS

We can use CSS to make our `<div>` tags look like the game board. CSS is a programming language that lets you change the way HTML elements display on your screen. You can change their size, shape, color, and position on the page.

An easy way to use CSS is to create a CSS class in the `<head>` of the page. The browser needs to know we are switching programming languages to CSS, so we have to use the `<style>` tag. Then we create a CSS class and apply it to the `<div>`. Look how easy it is to change the look of our page:

```html
<!DOCTYPE html>
<html>
    <head>
    <title>CSS</title>
    <style>
        .names {
            font-size: 16pt;
            text-align: center;
            background-color: blue;
        }
    </style>
    </head>
    <body>
        <div class="names">
            <p>Ruby</p>
            <p>Scratch</p>
        </div>
    </body>
</html>
```

style tag — `<style>`

CSS class name — `.names`

CSS property — `font-size`

CSS value — `16pt`

class attribute — `class=`

CSS class name — `"names"`

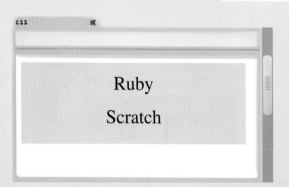

Here we have created a CSS class called names, which will change the font size, alignment, and background color of any HTML element it is applied to. Notice the dot (.) before the class name. We put all the CSS properties and values we want to use in the class inside braces ({ }).

To apply the CSS class, we add the class attribute to the element we want to change, then set the value of the attribute to the name of the CSS class. In this case, we want to apply the class to the `<div>`, so we have added the attribute to the opening `<div>` tag.

Did you notice?

To set the value of an attribute, you have to use the equals (=) sign and put the value inside straight (" ") quotes. If you use curly quotes, your code won't run.

CSS Properties and Values

Here are some more useful CSS properties and values. We will need to use these to create our game board.

Look at the different properties you can use in your code.

CSS property name	What does it mean?	Example values
height	Sets the height of the HTML element	100px; 100%;
width	Sets the width of the HTML element	100px; 100%;
border	Gives the HTML element a border	5px solid black;
padding	Creates white space around the HTML element	10px;
float	Positions the HTML element to the left or right of another element	left; right; none;
clear	Specifies which elements can float beside the HTML element and on which side	left; right; both;

The Lucky Cat Club is fun!

Now you can start coding your game board!

CODE WORDS Graphics on your computer screen are made up of tiny colored dots called **PIXELS** (px). You can tell your browser how many pixels you want to have in an HTML element.

26

GAME BUILD 1 ▶ THE GAME BOARD

Follow these steps to code the *Noughts and Crosses* game board using HTML and CSS.

1. Open your text-editing program. Go back to the Key Code Skills on pages 15–17 if you need a reminder about how to do this.

2. Type this code into your text-editing program:

```
<!DOCTYPE html>
<html>
    <head>
        <title>Noughts and Crosses</title>
        <style>
        </style>
    </head>
    <body>
        Click to play Noughts and Crosses.<br/>
    </body>
</html>
```

Copy the code carefully! Your browser won't be able to read the code if there are mistakes in it. Indenting every time you open a new tag will help make the block easier to read. Remember to close all the tags with a forward slash (/).

3. Save the file in your **Coding 2** folder as an HTML file (**.html**). Call it **OXO1.html**.
Go back to the Key Code Skills on page 16 if you need a reminder about how to do this.

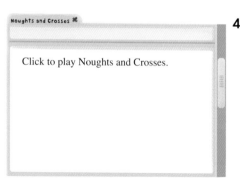

Noughts and Crosses

Click to play Noughts and Crosses.

4. Open the HTML file in your web browser. Go back to the Key Code Skills on page 17 if you need a reminder. The code will be displayed on-screen as a web page like this:

continues

5. Now that we've coded the basic structure of the web page, we need to make the board using `<div>` tags. Inside your `<body>` tag, code nine empty `<div>` tags. Each `<div>` will be a box on the board. Divide the nine elements into three groups of three using more `<div>` tags. Add the class attribute to those tags. Set the class value to row, like this:

```
<body>
  Click to play Noughts and Crosses.<br/>
  <div>
    <div class="row">
        <div></div>
        <div></div>
        <div></div>
    </div>
    <div class="row">
        <div></div>
        <div></div>
        <div></div>
    </div>
    <div class="row">
        <div></div>
        <div></div>
        <div></div>
    </div>
  </div>
</body>
```

6. Now add the row div CSS class to your `<style>` tag in the `<head>` of your page. You want the CSS class to change the padding, border, height, width, and float properties of your elements to the following values:

```
<style>
  .row div {
    padding: 10px;
    border: 1px solid black;
    height: 30px;
    width: 30px;
    float: left;
  }
</style>
```

We're telling our browser that whenever it sees a `<div>` tag with the class attribute row div, it should make the `<div>` 30 pixels wide and 30 pixels high. The browser should also put a 1-pixel solid-black border and 10 pixels of padding around the `<div>`, and make it float to the left of another element. This means that all the `<div>` tags inside each row of your game board will be positioned next to one another on our page. If you save the file and refresh the browser, the game board will look like this:

Noughts and Crosses ✖

Click to play Noughts and Crosses.

7. But we don't want nine boxes in a row! We need another CSS class to make the board display as a 3 x 3 grid. Inside your `<style>` tag, create another class called row, then use the clear property and set the value to both. This property will stop the groups of elements from floating to the left or right side of one another.

```
.row {
    clear: both;
}
</style>
```

8. Save your file and refresh your browser. Your game board will now look like this:

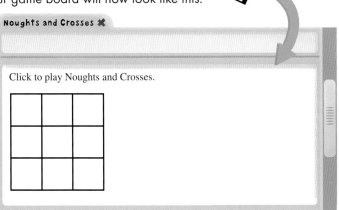

Noughts and Crosses ✖

Click to play Noughts and Crosses.

Now we need to make something happen when the players click on the boxes.

MAKING THE GAME INTERACTIVE

At the moment, if you try to click on the game board, nothing happens. We need to add code that will make the board into a game for the players. To do this, we have to use a third programming language, JavaScript, alongside the HTML and CSS. JavaScript makes web pages responsive. With JavaScript, a user can click on an HTML element and something will happen: an image will change, text will be displayed in a different way, or an element will be revealed or removed.

JavaScript is a great language for coding games because it means that the player can click on the page and see an instant result, making it an interactive experience. We are going to use JavaScript to make the X or the O appear on the game board when the player clicks on the `<div>` tags. But first we're going to learn some basic JavaScript syntax.

Using JavaScript

To add JavaScript to your game, you use the `<script>` tag to tell your browser you are switching languages. JavaScript is formed of pieces of code called statements. Each statement is an instruction for your browser. Statements always end with a semicolon (;) so your browser knows when the instruction has come to an end. Almost everything in JavaScript is an object, which has properties and methods we can access in our code. Here we have coded a JavaScript statement that tells the browser to pop up an alert containing a string of text.

```
<body>
    <script>
      alert("Get ready for the hackathon!");
    </script>
</body>
```

script tag

semicolon

JavaScript statement

Statements ✱

Get ready for the hackathon! ✕

OK

Did you notice?

The quotes in our code are always straight (" ") rather than curly (" "). Don't forget the semicolon (;) at the end of each statement.

30

Functions

Normally, we want to give the browser a set of instructions that is more complicated than a single JavaScript statement. We also might want the browser to perform that set of instructions in more than one place in our code. In order to create these more complicated sets of instructions, we use a function. A function is a group of JavaScript statements that run one after another to perform a certain action. You give your function a name that describes the action it performs. Once you have created (or defined) a function, you can use it as many times as you need to in your code. All you have to do is "call" the function using its name, like this:

```
<body>
  <script>
    function plan() {          function name
      alert("Get ready for the hackathon!");
      alert("Learn JavaScript!");
      alert("Code Noughts and Crosses!");
    }
    plan();          function call
  </script>
</body>
```

function keyword

function body

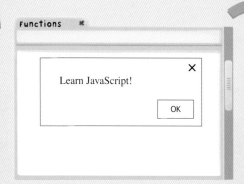

Here we have created a function named `plan`. All the JavaScript statements that we want to group together go inside the braces ({ }) and will be run one after another. In this piece of code, the `plan` function will make three different alerts pop up. To make the function run, we call it, and we do that by using the function name followed by a pair of parentheses (( )).

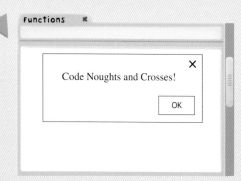

Arguments

Often we need to give a function a piece of information, or a value, to help it carry out the set of instructions. Giving a function a value is called passing it an argument. An argument can be used to change the way a function behaves when it is called. Take a look at this example:

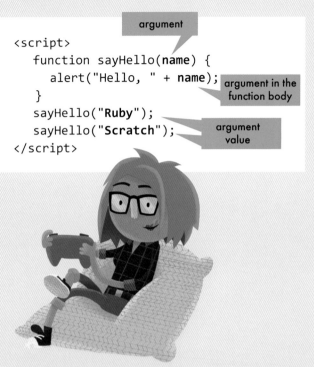

```
<script>
  function sayHello(name) {
    alert("Hello, " + name);
  }
  sayHello("Ruby");
  sayHello("Scratch");
</script>
```

argument

argument in the function body

argument value

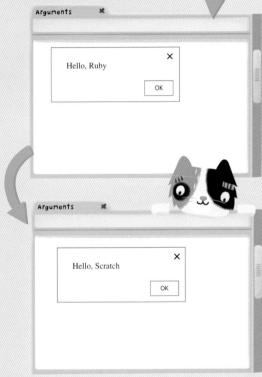

Every time we call the sayHello function, we are passing it the name argument, which forms part of the text of the pop-up alert. When we pass the value Ruby, the alert shows Ruby's name. And when we pass the value Scratch, the alert uses the same argument but shows Scratch's name instead. Using arguments allows us to be flexible with our functions, adapt them to different uses, and use them multiple times in our code.

The onclick Attribute

Now that we understand how functions and arguments work, we can use them in our game. We want a function to run when a player clicks in a box on the game board. The player has to be able to call the function in some way so the JavaScript will run.

We want the game board `<div>` tags to call a function when the player clicks on them. The best way to do this is to add the `onclick` attribute to the HTML elements you want to be interactive. The value of the attribute is the piece of JavaScript you want to run. When the user clicks on the HTML element, the JavaScript will run, like this:

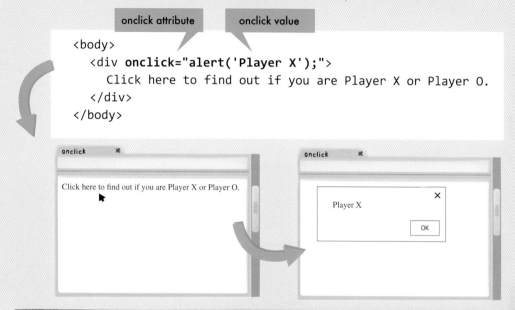

onclick attribute

onclick value

```
<body>
    <div onclick="alert('Player X');">
        Click here to find out if you are Player X or Player O.
    </div>
</body>
```

Click here to find out if you are Player X or Player O.

Player X

OK

The this Keyword

JavaScript keywords are special commands that your browser understands. One of these keywords is this. The this keyword allows you to point to something specific in your code without having to write it out again. Look at this example:

```
<script>
    function showCatName(name) {
        alert(name.innerText);
    }
</script>
<div onclick="showCatName(this)">Scratch</div>
```

this keyword

We are using the this keyword in the onclick attribute to refer to the value of the showCatName function. Using this allows us to make our code more accurate and flexible.

Scratch

Scratch

OK

GAME BUILD 2 ▶ ADDING JAVASCRIPT

Let's make the game board interactive using JavaScript and the `onclick` attribute.

1. Open up your saved **OXO1.html** file in your text-editing program. Add the `<script>` tag to your code block, underneath the code for the game board:

```
    </div>
    <script>
    </script>
  </body>
</html>
```

2. Now code a JavaScript function that will call an alert when a box on the game board is clicked. Call your function `place`, then pass it the argument box. In the function body, code an alert that will pop up a message. Put the function body inside braces ({ }). Don't forget that every JavaScript statement ends with a semicolon (;).

```
</div>
<script>
  function place(box) {
    alert("You clicked here!");
  }
</script>
```

> The braces keys are next to the P key on the keyboard. Press Shift to use them.

3. Now make the nine `<div>` tags that form the 3 x 3 grid interactive by adding `onclick` attributes. Set the value of the `onclick` to the name of your `place` function by typing inside the opening `<div>` tag as shown in the code block. Use the `this` keyword to refer to each of the boxes.

```
<div>
    <div class="row">
        <div onclick="place(this)"></div>
        <div onclick="place(this)"></div>
        <div onclick="place(this)"></div>
    </div>
    <div class="row">
        <div onclick="place(this)"></div>
        <div onclick="place(this)"></div>
        <div onclick="place(this)"></div>
    </div>
    <div class="row">
        <div onclick="place(this)"></div>
        <div onclick="place(this)"></div>
        <div onclick="place(this)"></div>
    </div>
</div>
```

4. Save your file as **OXO2.html** and open it in your browser. When you click on any of the nine boxes on the game board, an alert will pop up.

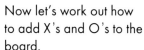

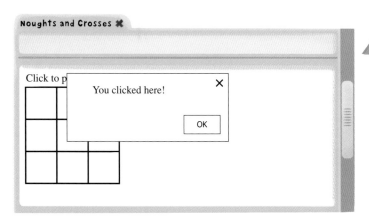

Noughts and Crosses ✖

Click to p

You clicked here! ✕

OK

Now let's work out how to add X's and O's to the board.

ADDING X'S AND O'S

We have built a game board that interacts with the player. But we want the board to do more than just pop up an alert. When a player clicks on a box, either an X or an O needs to be displayed inside it. We can use JavaScript to work out which player has had their turn and therefore whether an X or an O should be displayed in that box. This data is

known as the **game state**. We need to learn how to use variables and conditional statements to keep track of it.

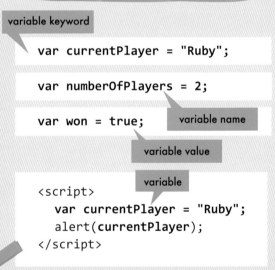

CODE WORDS — The **GAME STATE** is all the data the program needs to remember in order for the game to work correctly. This includes things such as the score, who the current player is, and where the enemies are.

Variables

We are going to use a variable to keep track of whose turn it is. A variable is a JavaScript container that stores a value. All you have to do is use the variable keyword var and give the variable a name of your choice. You set the value using the equals sign (=). This is called assigning a value. Strings of text are written in double quotes (" "). Numbers and Booleans are written without quotes.

Creating a variable allows us to access that value anywhere in our code. All you have to do is use the variable's name. Here we've passed the alert function the value of the variable as an argument:

variable keyword

```
var currentPlayer = "Ruby";

var numberOfPlayers = 2;

var won = true;
```
variable name

variable value

variable

```
<script>
    var currentPlayer = "Ruby";
    alert(currentPlayer);
</script>
```

As the name suggests, the value of a variable can vary, or change. The variable acts as a container for the value, and the value inside the container can change. So in this example, we could change the value stored in the currentPlayer variable to Markus. This changeability is useful because it gives us a way to make our code do different things depending on the value stored.

Variables ✱

Ruby ✕

OK

Remember: the value of a variable can change.

36

The DOM

An important part of our game is making sure that when a player clicks on an empty box, either an X or an O appears. The X or the O will be a new HTML element that we have added to the page after the game board has been drawn on-screen. To add a new HTML element, we need to use JavaScript to access a useful **API** called the DOM (Document Object Model).

The DOM allows us to connect our HTML web page to the JavaScript language. Using the DOM gives us a way in JavaScript to keep track of all the HTML elements that we've used to create the page, such as paragraphs, line breaks, and `<div>` tags.

We can use DOM methods and properties with JavaScript to access the HTML elements and make changes to them. A DOM method is an action you can perform on an HTML element. A DOM property is a value of an HTML property you can set or change. The DOM also allows us to do useful things like find, add, and delete HTML elements from our page. Using the DOM is simple. All you have to do is type the keyword:

`document.`

> **CODE WORDS** An **API** (Application Program Interface) is a program that allows two programs to connect and talk to each other. Every time you check the weather or send an instant message on your phone, you use an API to connect your phone to that data.

Using Dot Notation

To access the methods and properties of the DOM, we have to write our code using dot notation. The syntax we need is

dot notation

`object.property;`

All we have to do is use full stops between each keyword. A line of dot notation for our game looks like this:

object   dot notation

`document.getElementById("player");`

property or method

We can use dot notation to access the properties and methods of any object in JavaScript, not just the DOM.

Did you notice?

A practice called camelCase is a way to join two or more words to form one word. The first word starts with a lowercase letter, and the remaining words begin with an uppercase letter. We use camelCase to make our code easier to understand.

Using DOM Methods and Properties

The DOM has many useful built-in methods and properties to help us build our game, including allowing us to make our game turn-based. Using the DOM, each player can place either an X or an O inside the boxes on the board. To do this, we are going to use a DOM method called getElementById, which finds an element using its id attribute. Then we can use a DOM property called innerText to change the contents of the <div> to our chosen value:

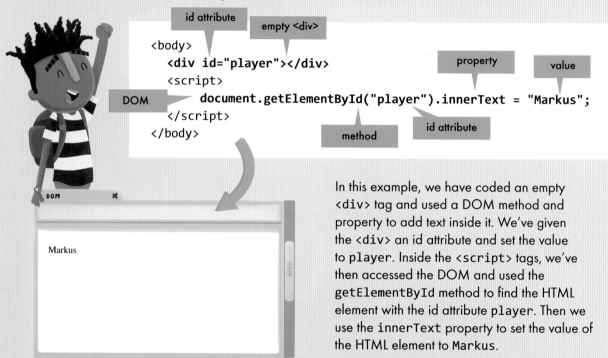

In this example, we have coded an empty <div> tag and used a DOM method and property to add text inside it. We've given the <div> an id attribute and set the value to player. Inside the <script> tags, we've then accessed the DOM and used the getElementById method to find the HTML element with the id attribute player. Then we use the innerText property to set the value of the HTML element to Markus.

If and Else Statements

Now that we know how to change the contents of an HTML element using the DOM, we have to find a way for the game to know whether an X or an O should be drawn inside the <div>. Let's learn how to use JavaScript conditionals. A conditional is a way of telling your browser that if something is true, it should perform an instruction. Otherwise,

the browser should do something else. Conditionals enable us to create code that can respond to different situations. There are two conditionals in JavaScript: if and else. An if statement executes a piece of code if something is true. Let's use an if statement to code an alert that will pop up if the person is a member of the Lucky Cat Club:

condition

equal to operator

keyword

```
<script>
    var member = "Ruby";
    if(member == "Ruby") {
        alert("Member of the Lucky Cat Club");
    }
</script>
```

code to execute if the condition is true

Here, the if statement is seeing if the value stored in the variable is true. We use the if keyword, then put the condition in brackets immediately afterward. We then use the equal to operator (==) to set the condition. Finally, we write the code that we want to run if the condition is true. We put this inside braces ({ }). In this case, we want an alert to pop up with a message.

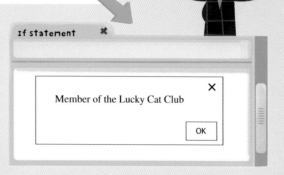

If statement ✖

Member of the Lucky Cat Club ✕

OK

Operator	Meaning
==	Equal to
!=	Not equal to

The second type of conditional is an else statement. With an else statement, we can instruct the browser to check if something is true. If it is false, the browser should execute another piece of code.

Turn the page to see how you can use if and else statements in your game build

condition

```
<script>
    var member = "SaberTooth Studios";
    if(member == "Ruby") {
        alert("Member of the Lucky Cat Club");
    }
    else {
        alert("Access denied!")
    }
</script>
```

else keyword

code to execute if the condition is false

Else statement ✖

Access denied! ✕

OK

Here, the value stored in the variable is not equal to the condition in the if statement. Because it is false, the else statement runs and a second alert pops up.

GAME BUILD 3 ► ADDING X'S AND O'S

Now that we understand variables, dot notation, and conditionals, let's use our new skills to add X's and O's to the game board.

1. Open up your saved **OXO2.html** file in your text-editing program. Add a variable to your `<script>` block before the function. Give the variable a name and set the value of the variable to the string O (the letter, rather than the number zero).

```
</div>
<script>
    var currentPlayer = "O";
    function place(box) {
        alert("You clicked here!");
    }
</script>
```

2. Delete the alert in your function. Replace it with a piece of code that sets the inner text of every `<div>` with the argument box to the value stored in the currentPlayer variable. The code you need looks like this:

```
<script>
    var currentPlayer = "O";
    function place(box) {
        box.innerText = currentPlayer;
    }
</script>
```

3. Then add an if statement to your function that will check whether a player should place an X or an O. The condition needs to ask if the currentPlayer is equal to (==) O. Next add the code to be executed if the condition is true. If an O has been placed on the board, the new currentPlayer is X. Code the following statement:

```
<script>
    var currentPlayer = "O";
    function place(box) {
        box.innerText = currentPlayer;
        if(currentPlayer == "O") {
            currentPlayer = "X";
        }
    }
</script>
```

4. Now add an else statement that will run if the condition is false. If the `currentPlayer` variable doesn't equal 0, it means that an X has been played. Therefore, the else statement needs to run and change the value of the variable to 0.

```
<script>
    var currentPlayer = "O";
    function place(box) {
       box.innerText = currentPlayer;
         if(currentPlayer == "O") {
            currentPlayer = "X";
         }
         else {
            currentPlayer = "O";
         }
    }
</script>
```

5. Save your file as **OXO3.html** and open in your browser. The first box you click in will display an O. The next box you click in will display an X.

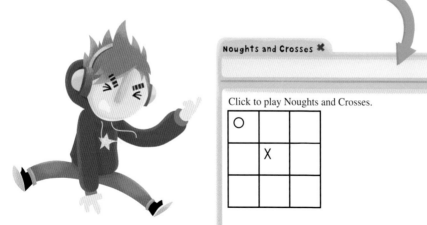

You will notice that there is a problem with your code. If you click on the same box twice, the O will change to an X and back again. We need to fix this, as it's against the rules of *Noughts and Crosses*.

CREATING TWO PLAYERS

When we click on the game board, an X or an O appears in each box. But when you click on the box again, the X or O will change. This is a **bug**. We need to learn how to stop the code from running once a player has clicked in the box. Then the next player can take their turn.

When you are coding, it is always good practice to try to make your block of code as simple and as short as possible. Let's also look at a clever way we can shorten the conditional statements in our code so the block is easier to understand.

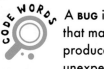
The return Keyword

To return from a function means to leave it and go back to the piece of code that called it. A function normally returns when it reaches the end of the final statement in the function body. But if you use the return keyword, it is possible to leave the function early.

We need to stop the if and else statements from constantly changing the value in the boxes when a player clicks. To do this, we need to add the return keyword to the place function at the point where we want it to stop running if there is text in the box:

```
<body>
  <div class="row">
      <div onclick="place(this)"></div>
  </div>
  <script>
      var currentPlayer = "O";
      function place(box) {
          if(box.innerText != "") return;
          box.innerText = currentPlayer;
          if(currentPlayer == "O") {
              currentPlayer = "X";
          }
          else {
              currentPlayer = "O";
          }
      }
  </script>
</body>
```

return keyword

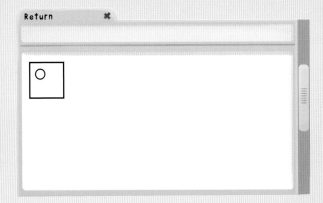

Here, we've added an if statement at the very start of our function. The condition asks if there is text in the box on our game board. We set the condition by asking if the `innerText` property is not equal to (!=) nothing (""). If the condition is true, and there is already text in the box, the `return` keyword will stop the rest of the function from being executed. Now the function runs only once, to add the O to the box. If we click on the box a second time, the function won't run.

Ternary Operator

We can write these if and else statements in a shorter way using a ternary operator. There are three parts to a ternary operator, and they always follow the same formula:

code to execute if false

```
condition ? then : otherwise;
```

condition

code to execute if true

We give the condition we want to test first, then the code we want to run if the condition is true, and finally the code we want to run if the condition is false. After the condition comes a question mark (?), and then the two code expressions are separated with a colon (:). Look how we can use the ternary operator to simplify this piece of code:

```
if(currentPlayer == "O") {
    currentPlayer = "X";
}
else {
    currentPlayer = "O";
}
```

into this far shorter line:

condition

code to execute if true

code to execute if false

```
currentPlayer == "O" ? currentPlayer = "X" : currentPlayer = "O";
```

Here, we are telling the browser that if the condition of the `currentPlayer` variable is equal to (==) O, then set the `currentPlayer` variable to X. Otherwise, if the condition is false, set it to O. Now the next player can take their turn.

Use the return keyword and a ternary operator to turn the game into something that two players can play.

1. Open up your saved **OXO3 .html** file in your text-editing program. Add a new if statement at the start of your function. Set the condition to ask if the innerText of all the <div> tags on the game board is empty. Then use the return keyword to stop the function from running if there is text in the <div> tags.

```
<script>
   var currentPlayer = "O";
   function place(box) {
      if(box.innerText != "") return;
      box.innertext = currentPlayer;
      if(currentPlayer == "O") {
         currentPlayer = "X";
      }
      else {
         currentPlayer = "O";
      }
   }
</script>
```

2. Now simplify the if and else statements into a ternary operator that decides whether an X or an O should be placed on the board. The code block for the entire <body> of your game will now look like this:

```
<body>
   Click to play Noughts and Crosses.<br/>
   <div>
      <div class="row">
         <div onclick="place(this)"></div>
         <div onclick="place(this)"></div>
         <div onclick="place(this)"></div>
      </div>
      <div class="row">
         <div onclick="place(this)"></div>
         <div onclick="place(this)"></div>
         <div onclick="place(this)"></div>
      </div>
```

```
    <div class="row">
        <div onclick="place(this)"></div>
        <div onclick="place(this)"></div>
        <div onclick="place(this)"></div>
    </div>
  </div>
  <script>
      var currentPlayer = "O";
      function place(box) {
          if(box.innerText != "") return;
          box.innerText = currentPlayer;
          currentPlayer == "O" ? currentPlayer = "X" : currentPlayer = "O";
      }
  </script>
</body>
```

3. Save your file as **OXO4.html** and open it in your browser. When you click on the boxes, an X or an O will appear in each. But when you click on a box a second time, the box will remain unchanged. Both players can play the game!

Now we need to figure out how to alert the winner and stop the game!

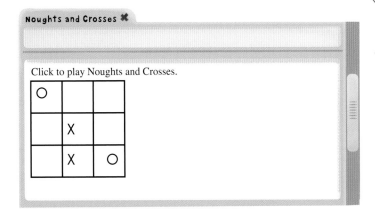

DETERMINING THE WINNER

Our game works, but if a player gets three in a row, there is no way of stopping the game and telling them they have won. We need to code a second function that will check every box on the game board to see if there is a winner. First we need to think about how our browser can identify each box on the game board.

Coordinates

Remember the rules of *Noughts and Crosses* at the start of the mission: you can win in three directions. If you place three X's or O's in an unbroken row horizontally, vertically, or diagonally, then you are the winner. To find out if a player has done this, we need to check the contents of each of the nine `<div>` tags that form the game board every time a player clicks.

To do this, we have to give each `<div>` tag an id attribute that represents its position on the board.

CODE WORDS **COORDINATES** are pairs of numbers taken from a horizontal (across) x-axis and a vertical (down) y-axis, and are a way to find a fixed position.

The best way to do that is to give each tag a set of **coordinates** that relate to its horizontal and vertical position. We give the horizontal position across the x-axis first, and then the vertical position down the y-axis. We arrange our coordinates like this:

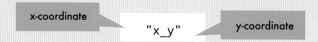

x-coordinate → "x_y" ← y-coordinate

If we look at a graph with axes, we can see how coordinates can be used to give a position:

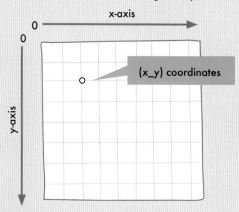

The x-coordinate refers to the position on the x-axis going across the screen horizontally, and the y-coordinate refers to the position on the y-axis going down the screen vertically.

0_0 <div>	1_0 <div>	2_0 <div>
0_1 <div>	1_1 <div>	2_1 <div>
0_2 <div>	1_2 <div>	2_2 <div>

Here's how we can give each of the <div> tags coordinates. The first number is the column number (going across the screen), and the second number is the row number (going down the screen). In computer science, we use zero-based numbering, which means the first row and column on the game board will be numbered zero rather than 1. So the <div> with the id attribute 1_0 will be the box in the second column and the first row on the game board.

Did you notice?

If you have used coordinates in math, you will have worked from the bottom left corner of the axes. However, when designing graphics on a computer, we work from the top left corner. This is because the first computers rendered graphics from the top of the screen.

Using id Attributes

We want to give each <div> its coordinates as an id attribute. Let's see how we would use coordinates and the id attribute to identify the first row of <div> tags on our game board:

```
<div class="row">                    id attribute
    <div id="0_0" onclick="place(this)"></div>
    <div id="1_0" onclick="place(this)"></div>
    <div id="2_0" onclick="place(this)"></div>
</div>
                    coordinates
```

Now we can use these id attributes to create a loop that will check all the <div> tags to see if we have a winner.

Using getElementById

We can use the getElementById method to find the <div> tags by their id attribute coordinates. As we saw on page 38, the method does exactly what its name suggests: it finds an HTML element by its id attribute. To use getElementById, we put the id attribute in parentheses, like this:

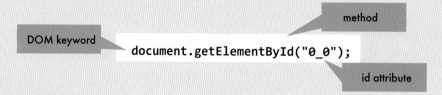

```
document.getElementById("0_0");
```

DOM keyword · method · id attribute

Let's code a simple example where we use getElementById to access the innerText of the first <div> in the first row, and find out if an X or an O is inside it. It will then pop up an alert showing the result:

```
<body>
  <div class="row">
    <div id="0_0">X</div>
  </div>
  <script>
    var first = document.getElementById("0_0");
    alert(first.innerText);
  </script>
</body>
```

id attribute · method · id attribute

Notice that we can use getElementById to create a value for a variable. This will be useful since we can then run an if statement that checks the condition of that variable.

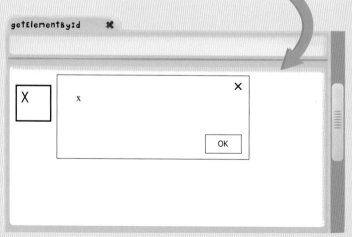

Looking good!

More Operators

We can use other operators to create more complicated if statements that check the condition of more than one variable at a time. This approach will help us store the X's and O's on the game board in variables using the getElementById method.

We can use the and operator (&&) to code an if statement that checks for three conditions. If all three conditions are true, it means there is a winner, because there are three of the same value in the <div> tags:

Operator	Meaning
&&	And

```
<script>
    var first = "X";
    var second = "X";
    var third = "X";
    if(first == second && first == third) {
        alert("Winner!");
    }
</script>
```

And operator

Here, we are asking the if statement to check if the first variable is equal to (==) the second variable and (&&) if the first variable is equal to (==) the third variable. If they are, an alert will pop up.

Hooray! You win!

Operators

Winner!

OK

GAME BUILD 5 ► DETERMINING THE WINNER

Use id attributes, coordinates, `getElementById`, and two new if statements to find out if there is a winner in the first row of the game board.

1. Open up your saved **OXO4.html** file in your text-editing program. Add an id attribute to each of the nine `<div>` tags on the game board. Set the value of each id attribute to the coordinate of that box on the board. Check back to page 47 to see the correct way to arrange coordinates.

```
<div>
  <div class="row">
    <div id="0_0" onclick="place(this)"></div>
    <div id="1_0" onclick="place(this)"></div>
    <div id="2_0" onclick="place(this)"></div>
  </div>
  <div class="row">
    <div id="0_1" onclick="place(this)"></div>
    <div id="1_1" onclick="place(this)"></div>
    <div id="2_1" onclick="place(this)"></div>
  </div>
  <div class="row">
    <div id="0_2" onclick="place(this)"></div>
    <div id="1_2" onclick="place(this)"></div>
    <div id="2_2" onclick="place(this)"></div>
  </div>
</div>
```

2. Now add a new `checkGameBoard` function that checks if there is a winner in the first row of the game board. Add it immediately after the `place` function. Code three variables to represent the first three boxes on the board. Use `getElementById` to access the text stored in each box. Store the value in the correct variable:

```
        currentPlayer == "O" ? currentPlayer = "X" : currentPlayer = "O";
}
function checkGameBoard() {
    var first = document.getElementById("0_0").innerText;
    var second = document.getElementById("1_0").innerText;
    var third = document.getElementById("2_0").innerText;
}
```

3. After the third variable, add two if statements. The first if statement needs to check if the first box is empty (""). This step is necessary because we don't want a player to win by doing nothing and having three empty boxes. We can use the return keyword to stop the code from running if there is nothing in the first variable box. The second if statement needs to check if all three boxes contain the same value. If they do, an alert saying "Winner!" should pop up:

```
    var third = document.getElementById("2_0").innerText;
    if(first == "") return;
      if(first == second && first == third) {
          alert("Winner!");
      }
}
```

4. Finally, call the new checkGameBoard function at the end of the previous place function. It should come after your ternary operator:

```
    currentPlayer == "O" ? currentPlayer = "X" : currentPlayer = "O";
    checkGameBoard();
}
```

5. Save your file as **OXO5.html** and open it in your browser. Click in the top row of the game board so that there are three O's. As you click to add the final O, an alert will pop up telling you that you are the winner. You can do the same in the top row with X's.

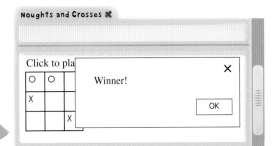

LOOPS

A player can now win the game by getting three O's or three X's in the first row. But what about the rest of the game board? We have to find a way to check the remaining boxes to see if there is a winner. To do this, we are going to code a loop.

Loops allow you to keep running a piece of code multiple times, depending on whether the condition is true or not. It's like saying that for as long as Scratch is hungry, Ruby should keep filling his bowl with cat food. When he's full, she should stop. In our game, we want the code to keep running for as long as it takes for a player to get three O's or X's in a winning formation. When the player gets three in a row, we want the code to stop.

For Loops

There are several different types of JavaScript loops. The one we need for our game is a for loop. This type of loop creates a variable, then loops around until the condition is true. At the end of each turn in the loop, the variable is updated. A for loop looks like this:

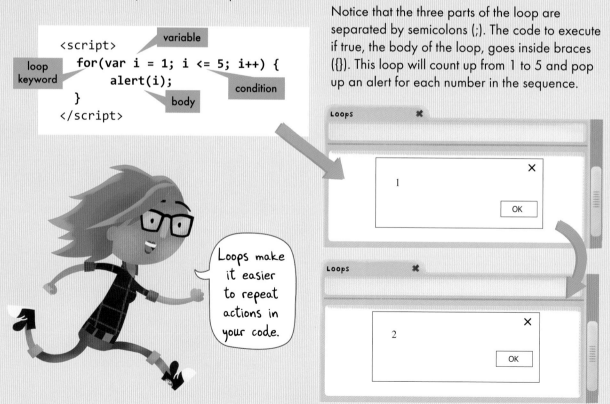

loop keyword

variable

```
<script>
    for(var i = 1; i <= 5; i++) {
        alert(i);
    }
</script>
```

body

condition

Notice that the three parts of the loop are separated by semicolons (;). The code to execute if true, the body of the loop, goes inside braces ({}). This loop will count up from 1 to 5 and pop up an alert for each number in the sequence.

LOOPS ✖

1

OK

LOOPS ✖

2

OK

Loops make it easier to repeat actions in your code.

52

The first part of the loop creates a variable with the value set to 1. The next part of the loop, the condition, checks if the variable is less than 5 using the less than or equal to (<=) operator. This is checked every time the loop runs, and if it is true, the body of the loop is executed. The increment operator (++) adds one to the value of the variable until we reach 5, and an alert pops up each time.

Operator	Meaning
++	Add one
>	Greater than
<	Less than
>=	Greater than or equal to
<=	Less than or equal to

Checking Rows

We can use a for loop in the checkGameBoard function to see if a player has won the game by getting three O's or three X's in a row. We want the loop to count upward through the game board <div> tags, using their id attributes:

```
function checkGameBoard() {
    for(var i = 0; i <= 2; i++) {
        var first = document.getElementById("0_" + i).innerText;
        var second = document.getElementById("1_" + i).innerText;
        var third = document.getElementById("2_" + i).innerText;
        if(first == "") continue;
        if(first == second && first == third) {
            alert("Winner!");
        }
    }
}
```

variable — condition — id attribute — variable — loop — continue keyword

We can change the function so that instead of asking the browser to find every coordinate on the board, a loop works out the row number each time. We then check all the rows on the board by passing getElementById the variable in the loop and the column part of the id attribute.

Checking Columns

We can use a second loop in the same way to determine if there are any winning combinations in the columns. All we have to do is switch around the way we check the `<div>` tags. At the moment, to check each row, we are using `getElementById` to find the boxes in the following way:

Remember how coordinates work. We need to reorder this piece of code so the loop is counting upward through the columns and adding them to the rows each time:

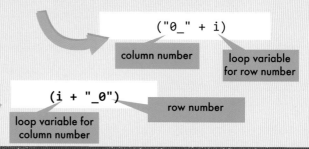

```
("0_" + i)
```
column number

loop variable for row number

```
(i + "_0")
```
loop variable for column number

row number

The continue Keyword

You may have noticed we are also using the continue keyword where we previously used return. Continue, when you use it in a loop, means skip to the next loop. It makes the loop continue without running any of the code after it.

How do I check the diagonals?

Checking Diagonals

We can't use a loop to check the diagonals, because both the row and the column numbers change. But luckily we know the id attributes for each of the boxes on the diagonals:

0_0	1_0	2_0
0_1	1_1	2_1
0_2	1_2	2_2

We can check the diagonals by coding a set of variables for each coordinate. Each of the six variables will store the value of the box using `getElementById`. Then we can use an if statement to check if there are three of the same value. Notice that we can use one if statement for each of the diagonals.

```
var firstD1 = document.getElementById("0_0").innerText;
var secondD1 = document.getElementById("1_1").innerText;
var thirdD1 = document.getElementById("2_2").innerText;
if(firstD1 != "" && firstD1 == secondD1 && firstD1 == thirdD1) {
    alert("Winner!");
}
var firstD2 = document.getElementById("0_2").innerText;
var secondD2 = document.getElementById("1_1").innerText;
var thirdD2 = document.getElementById("2_0").innerText;
if(firstD2 != "" && firstD2 == secondD2 && firstD2 == thirdD2) {
    alert("Winner!");
}
```

If statement

If statement

Each if statement means:

🐱 If the first box is not equal to (!=) nothing (" ") (it's not empty)

🐱 and (&&) the first diagonal is equal to (==) the second diagonal

🐱 and (&&) the first diagonal is equal to (==) the third diagonal,

🐱 then show the winner alert.

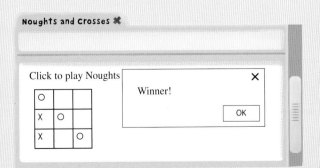

We're winning at the Game Build!

GAME BUILD 6 ► USING LOOPS TO CHECK THE BOARD

Use loops to keep checking the rows and columns of your game board until a player gets three in a row. Use conditionals to check the diagonals.

1. Open up your saved **OXO5.html** file in your text-editing program. Change your checkGameBoard function by adding a loop that will count through the rows on the board until there are three the same:

```
    function checkGameBoard() {
      for(var i = 0; i <= 2; i++) {
        var first  = document.getElementById("0_"+ i).innerText;
        var second = document.getElementById("1_"+ i).innerText;
        var third  = document.getElementById("2_"+ i).innerText;
        if(first == "") continue;
        if(first == second && first == third) {
           alert("Winner!");
        }
      }
    }
</script>
```

> Don't forget to update the coordinates and use the continue keyword too.

2. Then add a second loop to the checkGameBoard function that checks each column in the same way. Add it underneath the row loop. Remember to open and close all your braces correctly.

```
      for(var i = 0; i <= 2; i++) {
        var first  = document.getElementById(i + "_0").innerText;
        var second = document.getElementById(i + "_1").innerText;
        var third  = document.getElementById(i + "_2").innerText;
        if(first == "") continue;
        if(first == second && first == third) {
           alert("Winner!");
        }
      }
    }
</script>
```

3. Finally, at the end of the checkGameBoard function, add the variables and if statements to check the diagonals of the game board:

```
        var firstD1  = document.getElementById("0_0").innerText;
        var secondD1 = document.getElementById("1_1").innerText;
        var thirdD1  = document.getElementById("2_2").innerText;
        if(firstD1 != "" && firstD1 == secondD1 && firstD1 == thirdD1) {
            alert("Winner!");
        }
        var firstD2  = document.getElementById("0_2").innerText;
        var secondD2 = document.getElementById("1_1").innerText;
        var thirdD2  = document.getElementById("2_0").innerText;
        if(firstD2 != "" && firstD2 == secondD2 && firstD2 == thirdD2) {
            alert("Winner!");
        }
    }
</script>
```

4. Save your file as **OXO6.html** and open it in your browser. The winner alert will pop up if you get three X's or three O's in a vertical, horizontal, or diagonal line.

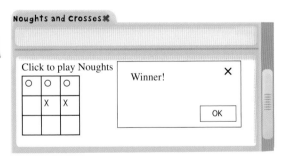

Look back at page 54 if you need a reminder about the coordinates.

SIMPLIFYING OUR CODE

Our code now works, but the complete block is long and repetitive. It's just doing the same thing over and over again. Let's see how we can write the same code in a shorter and simpler way. This is a good way to code. It makes your block easier for other people to read and understand.

Simplifying the If Statement

We can code a new checkWinner function at the end of our <script> block that checks for a winner without using so many different if statements. If we pass the new function for each of our three variables as arguments, it can apply the same if statement to them all:

function

arguments

```
function checkWinner(first, second, third) {
    if(first != "" && first == second && first == third) {
        alert("Winner!");
    }
}
```

We then need to call the new function at the end of each set of variables, like this:

```
var third  = document.getElementById("2_" + i).innerText;
checkWinner(first, second, third);
```

function call

arguments

I can't wait to play!

We've nearly finished our first game!

Simplifying the Loops

You may have noticed that at the moment our code is running two identical loops, one after another. Let's start by making the block shorter by using one loop to check both the rows and columns. We need to change the variable names throughout:

```
for(var i = 0; i <= 2; i++) {
    var rowFirst  = document.getElementById("0_" + i).innerText;
    var rowSecond = document.getElementById("1_" + i).innerText;
    var rowThird  = document.getElementById("2_" + i).innerText;
    checkWinner(rowFirst, rowSecond, rowThird);
    var colFirst  = document.getElementById(i + "_0").innerText;
    var colSecond = document.getElementById(i + "_1").innerText;
    var colThird  = document.getElementById(i + "_2").innerText;
    checkWinner(colFirst, colSecond, colThird);
}
```

new variable names

We can then simplify this even further. At the moment we are using a different variable for every <div> on the board, but we don't need to. We can pass the calls to getElementById as arguments in the checkWinner function. This block of code can be simplified from this:

```
var rowFirst  = document.getElementById("0_" + i).innerText;
var rowSecond = document.getElementById("1_" + i).innerText;
var rowThird  = document.getElementById("2_" + i).innerText;
checkWinner(rowFirst, rowSecond, rowThird);
```

to this:

```
checkWinner(document.getElementById("0_" + i).innerText,
            document.getElementById("1_" + i).innerText,
            document.getElementById("2_" + i).innerText);
```

Instead of using three variables to store the row information, we are using the innerText property to put the value of that <div> straight into the checkWinner function.

Did you notice?

Because we are passing multiple statements into the checkWinner function, we separate them using a comma (,) rather than a semicolon.

 **GAME BUILD 7** ► **SIMPLIFYING YOUR CODE**

Your game now works. All that's left is to tidy up your code.

1. Open up your
   OXO6.html file.
   Create a function
   at the end of your
   <script> block
   that uses one if
   statement to check
   for the winner.

```
    function checkWinner(first, second, third) {
        if(first != "" && first == second && first == third) {
            alert("Winner!");
        }
    }
</script>
```

2. Simplify the checkGameBoard function so that one loop checks both the rows and columns. Delete the variables you had used to store each <div>. Instead, pass the getElementById call into the function that checks the winner:

```
function checkGameBoard() {
    for(var i = 0; i <= 2; i++) {
        checkWinner(document.getElementById(i + "_0").innerText,
                    document.getElementById(i + "_1").innerText,
                    document.getElementById(i + "_2").innerText);
        checkWinner(document.getElementById("0_" + i).innerText,
                    document.getElementById("1_" + i).innerText,
                    document.getElementById("2_" + i).innerText);
    }
    checkWinner(document.getElementById("0_0").innerText,
            document.getElementById("1_1").innerText,
            document.getElementById("2_2").innerText);
    checkWinner(document.getElementById("0_2").innerText,
            document.getElementById("1_1").innerText,
            document.getElementById("2_0").innerText);
}
function checkWinner(first, second, third) {
```

3. Save your code as **OXO7.html** and open it in your browser. Your game will
   work in exactly the same way as before.

FINISHING THE GAME

The last thing we need to do is fix the bug that means even if a player has won, players can keep playing the game by clicking in the empty boxes. The game needs to end once a player has three in a row.

Edge Case

Edge case is a condition or situation that only happens very occasionally in a piece of code but produces a bug that stops it from running properly.

The situation in our game, where players can keep filling in the boxes even after someone has won, is an example of edge case. We need to

make sure our code can cope with this possibility, even if it is an unlikely scenario.

We need to update the code that checks for the winner to make sure it's keeping track of who's won. We do this by adding a new variable and using the or operator (||) in our place function:

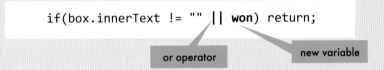

```
if(box.innerText != "" || won) return;
```

or operator   new variable

We're using the or (||) operator in the condition of the if statement. It will stop the code from running if the box is empty (" ") or (||) if the game has been won. The if statement can be broken down to read:

Operator	Meaning
||	Or

One more Game Build and we're finished!

> 🐱 If box.innerText is not equal to (!=) empty ("")
>
> 🐱 or (||) the game is won,
>
> 🐱 then return and stop running the code.

GAME BUILD 8 ► FINISHING THE GAME

Fix the final bug in your game and then get ready to play!

1. Open up your saved **OXO7.html** file in your text-editing program. Add a variable to the top of your `<script>` block that has the value `false`:

```
<script>
    var currentPlayer = "O";
    var won = false;
    function place(box) {
```

2. We then need to update the if statement in the function that checks for the winner so that when a player wins, the value of that new variable can be set to `true`:

```
function checkWinner(first, second, third) {
    if(first != "" && first == second && first == third) {
        alert("Winner!");
        won = true;
    }
}
```

3. Finally, at the top of the `place` function, we need to update the if statement to check if the game has already been won, using the or (||) operator:

```
function place(box) {
    if(box.innerText != "" || won) return;
```

4. Save your code as **OXO8.html** and open it in your browser. The game is now finished. We can play *Noughts and Crosses*. Why don't you find a friend to play with?

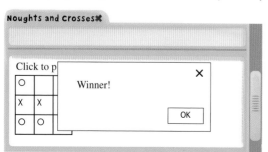

Congratulations!

SUPER SKILLS

Your game is ready to play! Let's think about how you can refine or adjust the design of the game board.

Taking your game further

- 🐱 Look at the CSS you've used to code the game board. Can you figure out how to change the CSS width and height properties to make the board bigger or smaller?

- 🐱 Can you change the background color of the board using the background-color CSS property?

- 🐱 Can you change the color of the X's and O's using the color CSS property?

- 🐱 Can you place the X's and O's in the middle of the boxes? (Hint: Use the text-align CSS property.)

- 🐱 You can also think about adding simple graphics to the game. How would you add a medal or trophy image using the image `<img>` tag and then using JavaScript to show or hide it?

- 🐱 Finally, if you're feeling really clever, try highlighting the winning row by setting the color CSS property of the winning cells.

Future game builds

With the skills you've learned from coding *Noughts and Crosses*, you can build other games that work on a turn-by-turn basis. Chess, checkers, and even big games like *Civilization* and Carcassonne are all turn-based games.

```html
<!DOCTYPE html>
<html>
    <head>
        <title>Noughts and Crosses</title>
            <style>
                .row div {
                    padding: 10px;
                    border: 1px solid black;
                    height: 30px;
                    width: 30px;
                    float: left;
                }
                .row {
                    clear: both;
                }
            </style>
    </head>
    <body>
        Click to play Noughts and Crosses.<br/>
        <div>
            <div class="row">
                <div id="0_0" onclick="place(this)"></div>
                <div id="1_0" onclick="place(this)"></div>
                <div id="2_0" onclick="place(this)"></div>
            </div>
            <div class="row">
                <div id="0_1" onclick="place(this)"></div>
                <div id="1_1" onclick="place(this)"></div>
                <div id="2_1" onclick="place(this)"></div>
            </div>
            <div class="row">
                <div id="0_2" onclick="place(this)"></div>
                <div id="1_2" onclick="place(this)"></div>
                <div id="2_2" onclick="place(this)"></div>
            </div>
        </div>
```

```
<script>
    var currentPlayer = "O";
        var won = false;
        function place(box) {
            if(box.innerText != "" || won) return;
            box.innerText = currentPlayer;
            currentPlayer == "O" ? currentPlayer = "X" : currentPlayer = "O";
            checkGameBoard();
        }
        function checkGameBoard() {
            for(var i = 0; i <= 2; i++) {
                checkWinner(document.getElementById(i + "_0").innerText,
                    document.getElementById(i + "_1").innerText,
                    document.getElementById(i + "_2").innerText);
                checkWinner(document.getElementById("0_" + i).innerText,
                    document.getElementById("1_" + i).innerText,
                    document.getElementById("2_" + i).innerText);
            }
                checkWinner(document.getElementById("0_0").innerText,
                    document.getElementById("1_1").innerText,
                    document.getElementById("2_2").innerText);
                checkWinner(document.getElementById("0_2").innerText,
                    document.getElementById("1_1").innerText,
                    document.getElementById("2_0").innerText);
        }
        function checkWinner(first, second, third) {
            if(first != "" && first == second && first == third) {
                alert("Winner!");
                won = true;
            }
        }
    </script>
  </body>
</html>
```

One game ready for the hackathon! Great coding!

65

SNAKE

- **LEARN TO USE THE ‹CANVAS› ELEMENT TO CREATE 2-D GRAPHICS**

- **ORGANIZE YOUR CODE WITH OBJECT LITERALS AND ARRAYS**

- **MAKE A GAME THAT TICKS**

- **LEARN HOW TO ADD AND PROCESS KEYBOARD INPUT**

Mission Brief

To | me@getcoding.com

CC | Ruby; Markus; Grace; Scratch

Subject | Mission 2 brief

Hey,

My name's Rusty and it's cool to meet you. I know you've already gotten an e-mail from Ruby telling you about the Lucky Cat Club. We've all been friends for ages, and we're really excited about learning to code. It's great that you are helping us get ready for the hackathon. I really hope we do well — and show those stuck-up coders at SaberTooth Studios that we're not to be messed with.

I think Ruby told you about *Tiger Trail*, SaberTooth's most famous game. The player has to direct a tiger around a game board and get it to eat as many deer as possible. When the tiger eats a deer, its body gets one stripe longer. As the player moves the tiger around the board, they have to be careful not to crash into any thornbushes. If they do, the game ends. The game has had almost a million downloads. People love it!

But the idea behind their game isn't actually one that the folks at SaberTooth thought up themselves. If you know anything about really old cell phones, you might have heard of the game *Snake*. It was one of the first games you could play on a phone, and it was *so* basic — it was 2-D, the graphics were black-and-white, and there were no sound effects or cool stuff. You had to make the snake grow by having it eat apples placed at random points on the board. And you had to keep it from crashing into the walls on the board or its own tail.

I want to learn how to code *Snake*. If SaberTooth can transform it into a best-selling game, I think I can give it a try. I'd like to know how to build more puzzle games in the future, so learning how *Snake* works seems like a good place to start. I'm hoping you can help me crack it before I get my tail in a tangle.

Purr-fect wishes,

Rusty

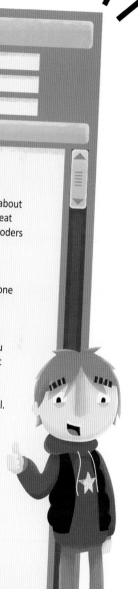

Snake

THE DEVELOPER'S
DICTIONARY
Your Guide to Games and
Gaming

Home page
Contents
Featured game
Gaming strategy
Build tips

From the Developer's Dictionary: Your Guide to Games and Gaming

This entry is about the game Snake. For other similar games, see Arcade Games.

Snake is the name for a common computer-game concept, with different versions available in <u>arcades</u>, on <u>computers</u>, and on different <u>platforms</u> for <u>phones</u> or <u>tablets</u>.

The <u>gameplay</u> of a Snake game is very simple. The player moves a straight line (the snake) around a board using their <u>keyboard</u>. Pieces of fruit or bugs appear in the game over time, and the player is supposed to make the snake eat the fruit or

Snake

Genre:	Puzzle
Mode:	Single-player
First release:	1976 (as Blockade)
Playing time:	1 minute or more (level-dependent)
Skills required:	Strategy, quick reactions, and observation

bugs by moving it into them. Every time the snake eats a piece of fruit or a bug, the player scores a point and the snake grows, making the game more difficult. The aim of the game is to score as many <u>points</u> as possible without letting the snake crash into a wall on the board or its own tail.

The Snake game concept was first made popular in 1976, as an arcade game called <u>*Blockade*</u>. The player had to move a character that left a solid black line behind it around the screen, using four buttons to determine the line's <u>direction</u>. The aim was to avoid hitting an <u>opponent</u>.

The popularity of *Blockade* led to lots of companies creating their own versions. Well-known ones include <u>*Worm*</u>, <u>*Nibbler*</u>, and <u>*Rattler Race*</u>. By far the most famous version, which was called *Snake*, came for free on <u>Nokia</u> cell phones in 1998. It was so popular that Nokia created multiple versions with increasing sophistication and complexity. *Snake II*, released on the <u>Nokia 3310</u>, is the best known.

Today there are a huge number of different games that use the Snake concept in some way, and it is often ranked as one of the top one hundred game types of all time.

SNAKE

We're going to code our own version of a Snake game that will run in a web browser rather than on a phone. We are going to use JavaScript to make the snake move and the fruit appear on the board, and an HTML element called <canvas> to create the simple game-board graphics.

We haven't used the <canvas> element before, so before we begin the Game Builds, we'll look at how it works in a Code Skills exercise. Then, just as in Mission 1, follow the step-by-step instructions in the Game Builds. By the end of the mission, you will be able to play your own Snake game.

The Game Build

To make our Snake game into a challenge for the player, we need to code a game board with different obstacles. The player will control the snake's movement using the keyboard and must keep it from crashing into the walls around the board and the island in the middle. Every few seconds, a fruit will appear in a random spot on the board. When the snake collides with the fruit, it will eat it and grow a section longer. The player scores a point for every fruit the snake eats. If the snake crashes into the walls, the island, or its own tail, the game ends and a pop-up alert tells the player the score.

At the end of the mission, your finished game will look like this:

Let's make SaberTooth Studios hiss-tory!

Snake

snake

walls

island

Game over! Player scored: 1

score alert

OK

fruit

CREATING GRAPHICS

To code the game board, we need to use the **HTML5** <canvas> element, which is used with JavaScript to draw graphics in a web browser. The <canvas> element works as a container that stores the graphics you create with JavaScript. Imagine the <canvas> element as a blank piece of paper and JavaScript as the paint.

You can create all kinds of graphics with the <canvas> element. Use it to draw circles, squares, and lines or to add text and images. For our version of *Snake,* we only need very simple graphics. The shapes we are going to draw with the <canvas>, in a process called rendering, are squares of varying sizes.

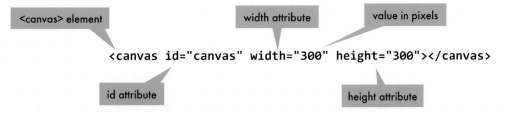

CODE WORDS

HTML5 is a version of the HTML programming language. It's the first version to include the <canvas> element.

Using the <canvas> Element

The <canvas> element works in the same way as the other HTML tags you have used so far. We set its width and height in pixels using attributes, and also give the element an id attribute so we can find it in our code. We create the <canvas> like this:

<canvas> element · width attribute · value in pixels

```
<canvas id="canvas" width="300" height="300"></canvas>
```

id attribute · height attribute

In order to use the <canvas> element with JavaScript, we have to access it using the DOM and getElementById. We can then assign the element to a variable:

variable · DOM · method · id attribute

```
var canvas = document.getElementById("canvas");
```

There are several <canvas> APIs that can be used with the element to create different effects on-screen. (Turn to page 37 for a reminder about the DOM and APIs.) Let's find out more.

Using getContext

By itself, the `<canvas>` element does nothing. It just acts as a container. To actually create the graphics on-screen, we need to access another JavaScript method: the drawing context. The drawing context provides all the methods and properties—the painting tools—to create the graphics you need.

To access the drawing context, we use `getContext`, which gives us the methods and properties we need for drawing on the `<canvas>`. We store the drawing context in a variable, so we can access it anywhere in our code:

context variable

getContext method

argument

```
var ctx = canvas.getContext("2d");
```

We've passed `getContext` the argument 2d because we want to make our game board from 2-D, or two-dimensional, shapes. This means the shapes will appear on-screen with a width and a height, but no depth.

Drawing Shapes

Now that we can access the drawing context, we want to use the `getContext` method to draw shapes on the `<canvas>`. We can use various methods and properties to create the shapes we need for the game board. Our game board is going to be made of lots of squares, so let's look at how we can draw a filled-in square.

Property	What does it do?
fillStyle	Sets the color used to fill in the drawing

To use the `fillStyle` property to change the color of a shape, we simply pick a color. There are over a hundred different color names to choose from, so don't be afraid to try different ones.

Find more color values on the Get Coding! website.

context

fillStyle property

value

```
ctx.fillStyle = "blue";
```

The `fillRect` method creates a filled-in shape with straight sides. You have to pass the method four arguments: the x- and y-coordinates to draw the shape from, and the width and the height of the shape.

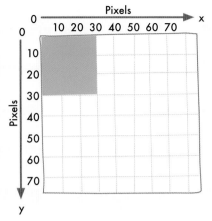

Method	What does it do?
fillRect	Draws a "filled" square
clearRect	Clears the specified pixels within a given rectangle

As we learned in Mission 1, coordinates can be used to give a position on-screen. Normally, one coordinate represents one pixel. As before, the coordinates are taken from the top left corner and arranged as x_y (the position across the screen, the position down the screen). In this example, we have set the coordinates to (0_0), so the rectangle is positioned in the top left corner. Here, we're setting the width and height attributes to 30 pixels, creating a square:

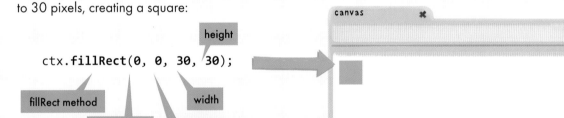

Removing Shapes

If we want to remove a shape from the `<canvas>`, the `clearRect` method follows the same rules as the `fillRect` method:

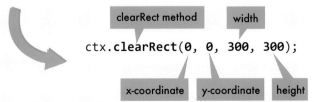

Here, the `clearRect` method will remove anything drawn on the `<canvas>` from the coordinates 0_0, which is the top left of our `<canvas>`, for 300 x 300 pixels, the size of our entire `<canvas>`.

Learn how to use the <canvas> element with JavaScript to draw and remove a square from your screen.

1. Open your text-editing program. Make a new file called **canvas.html**. Use the <canvas> element to create a canvas measuring 300 x 300 pixels:

> Don't forget to add the id attribute so you can use the element later in your code.

```
<!DOCTYPE html>
<html>
    <head>
        <title>Canvas</title>
    </head>
    <body>
        <canvas id="canvas" width="300" height="300"></canvas> <br/>
    </body>
</html>
```

2. Now let's add two buttons to the page, using <input> tags. Set their onclick attributes to call a draw and a remove function. We'll code the functions in the next steps. (Turn to page 31 if you need a reminder about functions.)

```
<!DOCTYPE html>
<html>
    <head>
        <title>Canvas</title>
    </head>
    <body>
        <canvas id="canvas" width="300" height="300"></canvas> <br/>
        <input type="button" onclick="draw()" value="Draw"/> <br/>
        <input type="button" onclick="remove()" value="Clear"/> <br/>
    </body>
</html>
```

3. Start a `<script>` block underneath the `<input>` tags. Use the `getElementById` method to find the `<canvas>` and then store it in a variable. Access the drawing context and store it in a second variable:

```
<script>
    var canvas = document.getElementById("canvas");
    var ctx = canvas.getContext("2d");
</script>
</body>
```

4. Now code the draw function that we called in step 2. Inside the function, use the drawing context to draw a black rectangle that's 30 x 30 pixels from the top left corner of the screen. You need to use the `fillStyle` property and the `fillRect` method, which takes four arguments:

```
function draw() {
    ctx.fillStyle = "black";
    ctx.fillRect(0, 0, 30, 30);
}
</script>
```

You can use whatever color you like in the `fillStyle` property, and you can change the `fillRect` arguments to make a different-size rectangle.

5. After the draw function, add a remove function that clears the square from the screen once it's been drawn. Use the `clearRect` method, like this:

```
function remove() {
    ctx.clearRect(0, 0, 300, 300);
}
</script>
```

6. Save your file and open it in your browser. When you click on the *Draw* button, a square will be drawn on-screen. When you click on the *Clear* button, the square will vanish.

Try using different colors.

THE GAME BOARD

Now that we know how to use the `<canvas>` element with JavaScript to create shapes, we need to build the game board. We are going to look at how we can use an array to draw the walls and the island obstacle on the `<canvas>`.

Arrays

We're going to use an array of strings to create the obstacles on the game board. In JavaScript, a string is used to represent characters that aren't numbers or Booleans. It's simple to store a string in a variable:

> **variable**   **string**
>
> `var luckyCatClub = "Ruby";`

But what do we do if we want to store more than one string value in a variable? We have to create a special kind of variable called an array. An array can hold as many values as you need. To access the individual values, you use a number known as an **offset**. Here is an array containing several different strings:

> **bracket**   **comma**
>
> `var luckyCatClub = ["Ruby", "Markus", "Grace", "Rusty"];`
>
> **array name**   **string 0**   **string 1**   **string 2**   **string 3**

To create an array, you have to put the values in brackets ([ ]) and separate them with commas. This array contains four strings. Arrays can be on multiple lines and contain characters other than letters, such as symbols and spaces.

We are going to use strings to create the obstacles on the game board. Hash characters (#) will represent the squares that make the walls and island. Space characters will represent the clear area the snake can move around in. Our board array will look like this:

> **x offset 0**   **string**
>
> ```
> var board = [ "###############",
>               "#            #",
>               "#            #"
>           ];
> ```
>
> **y offset 1**   **hash character**   **space character**

CODE WORDS — An **OFFSET** is the distance in an array from the beginning to a given element or point within it. The offset starts from zero and uses x- and y-coordinates.

Did you notice?

There is no comma after the last value in the array.

The forEach Method

We can use the forEach method to call a function on each string in an array, in order. It means we can use the same function multiple times. You use forEach like this:

array name · function keyword · argument

```
array.forEach(function name(currentValue));
```

forEach method · function name

Look at how we can use forEach to call a function on every item in the luckyCatClub array:

```
<script>
    var luckyCatClub = [
        "Rusty",
        "Grace",
        "Markus",
        "Ruby"
    ];
    luckyCatClub.forEach(function sayName(name) {
        alert(name);
    });
</script>
```

array · forEach method · argument · function name

When you run this code, forEach calls the sayName function for every string in the luckyCatClub array. The function pops up an alert to show the value for each of the strings in the order they are written in the array.

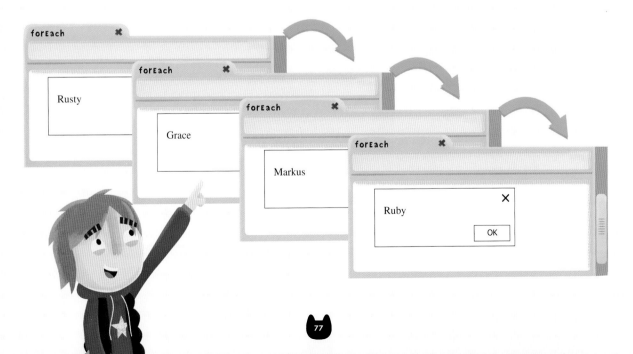

The Split Method

We can also split the individual strings in the array. To do this, we use the split method, which breaks the string into smaller parts. You use split like this:

string name | how to split the string

```
string.split(separator);
```

split method

Let's look at an example where we call the split method with an empty string (' '), so the string is split into individual characters:

```
<body>
    <p>Click the button to see the array values after the split.</p>
    <button onclick="splitString()">Try it</button>
    <p id="answer"></p>
    <script>
        function splitString() {
            var string = "Lucky Cat Club";
            var value = string.split('');
            document.getElementById("answer").innerHTML = value;
        }
    </script>
</body>
```

split method

separator

string to split

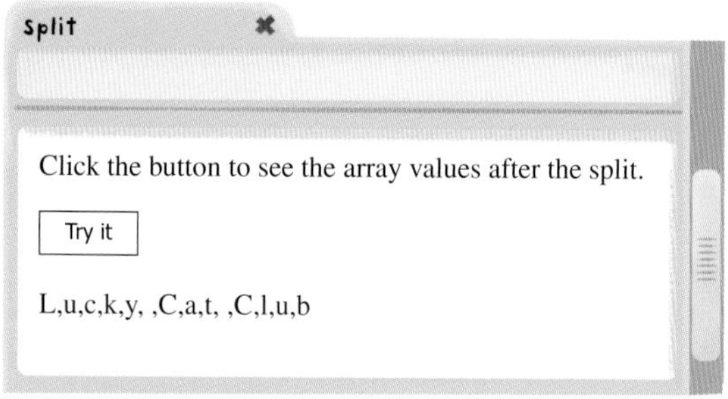

Split ✖

Click the button to see the array values after the split.

Try it

L,u,c,k,y, ,C,a,t, ,C,l,u,b

The Lucky Cat Club are coding champions!

Now let's see how we can use an array with the forEach and split methods to draw the game board on-screen.

78

Using an Array to Create the Game Board

Once we have created our board array using the hash (#) and space characters, we can use the `split` and `forEach` methods to access each character in the strings. We can create a function and use `forEach` to check each line of the board array. The function will split each string in the array into individual characters. Then we can call a second function on each individual character. If the character is a hash (#), we use the `<canvas>` APIs to render it as a black square on-screen:

```
board.forEach(function checkLine(line) {
    line = line.split('');
    var currentXoffset = 0;
    line.forEach(function checkCharacter(character) {
        if(character == '#') {
            ctx.fillStyle = "black";
            ctx.fillRect(currentXoffset, currentYoffset, squareSize, squareSize);
        }
        currentXoffset += squareSize;
    });
    currentYoffset += squareSize;
});
```

array   forEach   checkLine function   split   offset   checkCharacter function   addition assignment operator

We want the squares to be drawn immediately after each other, with no break between them, so we are keeping track of the offset position across the x-axis. We can then use the addition assignment operator (+=) to add the current x offset position to the square size. This gives us the width of the last square rendered on-screen, so as we move across every character, we draw the next square immediately to the right of it.

After rendering every line, we're then adding the current y offset position to the square size, so that when we loop around to the next string, we're drawing the new squares underneath the line we've just rendered.

This is your game board.

79

Use `<canvas>`, an array, and the `forEach` and `split` methods to create the game-board graphics.

1. Start by creating a new file called **snake1.html**. Code the basic structure of an HTML page. Then add the `<canvas>` element and set the id, height, and width attributes, like this:

```
<!DOCTYPE html>
<html>
    <head>
        <title>Snake</title>
    </head>
    <body>
        <canvas id="canvas" width="1024" height="1024"></canvas>
    </body>
</html>
```

2. Underneath the `<canvas>`, create an array to define the game board. Use the hash character (#) for the walls and island, and use the space character for the space on the board the snake can move in. The walls are 15 hash characters wide and 10 high.

```
<script>
    var board = [
        "###############",
        "#             #",
        "#             #",
        "#             #",
        "#      ####    #",
        "#      ####    #",
        "#             #",
        "#             #",
        "#             #",
        "###############"
    ];
</script>
```

> Remember to place a comma after each string in the array except the final one and to put the array in brackets ([ ]).

3. Below the array, use the getElementById method to find the <canvas> and store it in a variable. Set the drawing context of the <canvas> to 2-D, like this:

```
var canvas = document.getElementById("canvas");
var ctx = canvas.getContext("2d");
</script>
```

4. Add a variable that keeps track of the position of the last square we added to the <canvas> on the y axis. Add a second variable to keep track of the width and height of each square. We want each square to be 30 x 30 pixels.

```
var currentYoffset = 0;
var squareSize = 30;
</script>
```

5. Now code a function that uses the forEach and split methods to break each string in the board array into individual characters. Then code a function that checks the individual characters. Use an if statement so that if the character is a hash (#), a black square is rendered on-screen. Keep track of the x and y offsets.

```
var squareSize = 30;
board.forEach(function checkLine(line) {
    line = line.split('');
    var currentXoffset = 0;
    line.forEach(function checkCharacter(character) {
        if(character == '#') {
            ctx.fillStyle = "black";
            ctx.fillRect(currentXoffset, currentYoffset, squareSize, squareSize);
        }
    currentXoffset += squareSize;
    });
    currentYoffset += squareSize;
});
</script>
```

6. Save your file and open it in your browser. The game board should look like this:

ORGANIZING THE GAME BOARD

As the game begins to grow, organizing the different functions and variables into object literals is a good way for us to make sure our code stays readable. So far, we've used variables and arrays to store data in our code. We can also use object literals to group related pieces of code. Each object literal needs a name so we can easily access the data inside it.

Object Literals

Object literals are similar to arrays. But while arrays allow us to list lots of different things (like the four members of the Lucky Cat Club), object literals allow us to represent one thing that has several different characteristics. For example, you probably have a first name, a last name, and a nickname. So far, if we want to store these pieces of information in our code, we've created three different variables:

```
var firstName = "Russel";
var lastName = "Eich";
var nickname = "Rusty";
```

object literal name

```
var person = {
    firstName: "Russel",
    lastName: "Eich",
    nickname: "Rusty"
};
```

name   value

Instead of having each of these variables separately in your code, you can use an object literal to collect them tidily in one place. For object literals, we use braces ({ }) instead of the brackets ([ ]) we use to create an array. Everything inside the braces is part of the object literal. Any data type can go in an object literal, including arrays, functions, and even other object literals.

Properties

The pieces of information inside the object are known as properties and they come in pairs: the name and the value. The name goes before the colon (:), and the value goes after. The name will always be a string, but the value can be anything you want. Each pair except the final one is followed by a comma.

To access the properties in an object, we have to code: **`objectName.property`**

So to use the value stored as Rusty's nickname, we would write: `person.nickname`

Using object literals allows us to group related pieces of data. Here we have all the variables and functions related to a person grouped into one tidy object literal:

```
var person = {
    firstName: "Russel",        variable
    lastName: "Eich",
    nickname: "Rusty",          function
    sayHello: function Hello(){
        alert(person.nickname + " " + person.lastName);
    }
};
person.sayHello();              function call
```

object literal

Objects ✖

```
Rusty Eich                    ✕

                    OK
```

Namespacing

When we create our object literals, it's important to make sure they are properly organized. Similar things should be grouped, and the group given a name. We call this namespacing. Using the namespace, we can then easily access the variables and functions inside the object literal anywhere in our code. Look how we've created a namespace for Scratch, gathering all the different functions relating to him:

This is a great way to group our functions.

namespace

```
var scratch = {
    meow: function() {…},
    eatCatFood: function() {…},
    playWithRuby: function() {…}
};
scratch.eatCatFood();
```

83

Use object literals to group related pieces of code.

1. Open up your **snake1.html** file. Let's put everything after the board array into an object literal called graphics. Inside the new object, organize your code into a new drawBoard function.

```
var graphics = {
    drawBoard: function() {
    var canvas = document.getElementById("canvas");
. . .
};
```

Remember to open and close the braces.

2. We can tidy up our code further. Remove <canvas> and squareSize from the drawBoard function, but keep them inside the graphics object. That way, in the future, all the functions we add to the object can use them. Update the drawBoard function so <canvas> and squareSize use the new namespace.

```
var graphics = {
    canvas: document.getElementById("canvas"),
    squareSize: 30,
    drawBoard: function() {
        var ctx = graphics.canvas.getContext("2d");
        var currentYoffset = 0;
        board.forEach(function checkLine(line) {
        line = line.split('');
        var currentXoffset = 0;
        line.forEach(function checkCharacter(character) {
            if(character == '#') {
                ctx.fillStyle = "black";
                ctx.fillRect(currentXoffset, currentYoffset, graphics.
squareSize, graphics.squareSize);
            }
            currentXoffset += graphics.squareSize;
        });
            currentYoffset += graphics.squareSize;
        });
    }
};
```

Notice that we've changed the code from canvas to graphics.canvas and from squareSize to graphics.squareSize.

3. Because we've moved the code into the new drawBoard function, we're going to need to add a function call for the code to run. Add a line after the graphics object to call the drawBoard function:

```
graphics.drawBoard();
```

4. Let's tidy up the board array by putting it in a game object:

```
var game = {
    board: [
        "###############",
        "#             #",
        "#             #",
        "#             #",
        "#    ####     #",
        "#    ####     #",
        "#             #",
        "#             #",
        "#             #",
        "###############"

    ]
};
```

Catch me if you can!

5. Make sure you change your checkLine function to use the new namespace:

```
board.forEach(function checkLine(line) {
```

```
game.board.forEach(function checkLine(line) {
```

6. Save your file as **snake2.html** and open it in your browser. Your game board should look exactly the same, but your code is now nice and tidy.

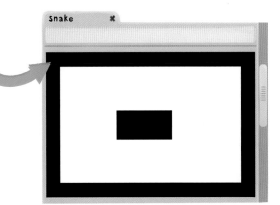

ADDING THE SNAKE

The snake in our game has three parts: the head, the middle, and the tail, which grows each time it eats a fruit. We need to be able to keep track of the snake and control each part of it in our code.

Structuring the snake

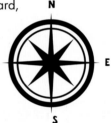

We are going to store information about the snake's three parts in our code. First we need to create an object literal that groups everything to do with our snake. Then we can create an array that breaks the snake down into three objects.

Which direction should the snake go?

We are giving each part of the snake two properties. These will relate to its x- and y-coordinates on the board. (Remember: the x-coordinate indicates an object's position across the board, and the y-coordinate indicates its position down the board.) First we want to get our snake to move from left to right across the board, so our x-coordinate will change but our y-coordinate will stay the same.

We're also adding a property that will enable us to control the snake's direction. This property will use the points of the compass: north, south, east, and west. We want the snake to move from left to right, so it will be facing east. Our code will look like this:

```
var snake = {        array    head object
    parts: [
object    {x: 4, y: 2},    middle object
        {x: 3, y: 2},
        {x: 2, y: 2}    tail object
    ],
    facing: "E"
};        direction property
```

N
W   E
S

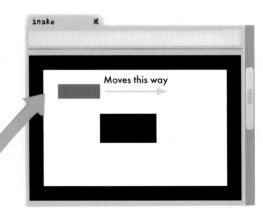

Snake ✕

Moves this way

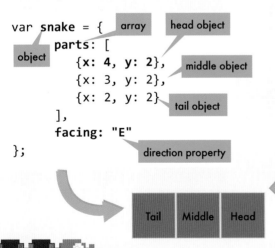

Tail | Middle | Head

This is how you code the snake!

86

Drawing the Snake

Now that we have the structure of the snake, it needs to be rendered on the board in the correct place. We need a drawSnake function that works in a similar way to the function that draws the board:

array

multiplication operator

object

<canvas> APIs

```
drawSnake: function () {
    var ctx = graphics.canvas.getContext("2d");
    snake.parts.forEach(function drawPart(part) {
        var partXlocation = part.x * graphics.squareSize;
        var partYlocation = part.y * graphics.squareSize;
        ctx.fillStyle = "green";
        ctx.fillRect(partXlocation, partYlocation, graphics.squareSize,
graphics.squareSize);
    });
}
```

The only difference is the way we are keeping track of the snake's parts in the drawPart function. We are accessing the head, middle, and tail objects one at a time and keeping track of the sequence. We're then using a simple calculation to work out where the snake should be drawn on-screen. And by changing the fillStyle and fillRect, we get a green snake.

The Math

We're using math to work out where the snake should be drawn on the board. To work out where we draw the three parts, we're using the x- and y-coordinates of each part, then multiplying them by the size of the squares. We use the multiplication operator (*) to do this.

This calculation works because we know that all our squares are the same size (30 x 30 pixels). For example, the tail object at location {x: 2, y: 2} would be in the following position:

part.x	multiplied by	squareSize	=	partXLocation
2	x	30	=	60
part.y	multiplied by	squareSize	=	partYLocation
2	x	30	=	60

So the tail should be drawn 60 pixels from the left of the canvas and 60 pixels from the top.

GAME BUILD 3 ▶ ADDING THE SNAKE

Create the snake and code a function that will draw it on the board.

1. Open up your **snake2.html** file. Create an empty object literal for the snake underneath the game object:

```
var snake = {
};
```

Let's add that snake!

2. Now create an array of three object literals to represent each part of the snake. Set an x and y property for each part. Also add a property that controls the direction of the snake:

```
var snake = {
    parts: [
        {x: 4, y: 2},
        {x: 3, y: 2},
        {x: 2, y: 2}
    ],
    facing: "E"
};
```

3. Inside the graphics object, underneath the drawBoard function, create a new function that will draw the snake:

```
    drawSnake: function() {
        var ctx = graphics.canvas.getContext("2d");
        snake.parts.forEach(function drawPart(part) {
            var partXlocation = part.x * graphics.squareSize;
            var partYlocation = part.y * graphics.squareSize;
            ctx.fillStyle = "green";
            ctx.fillRect(partXlocation, partYlocation, graphics.
squareSize, graphics.squareSize);
        });
    },
};
graphics.drawBoard();
```

Don't forget to add a comma after the brace at the end of your drawBoard function above!

4. Now that we have a function for drawing the snake, let's make sure we call it. Add the function call under the drawBoard call:

```
graphics.drawBoard();
graphics.drawSnake();
```

5. Now move the two function calls that draw the snake and the board into the graphics object, and create a new drawGame namespace that groups them together. Then call the new function:

```
var graphics = {
    . . .
    drawGame: function () {
        graphics.drawBoard();
        graphics.drawSnake();
    }
};
graphics.drawGame();
</script>
```

6. We can make the block even tidier by calling getContext only once in our new drawGame function and passing it as an argument at different points in our code:

```
var graphics = {
    canvas: document.getElementById("canvas"),
    squareSize: 30,
    drawBoard: function(ctx) {
        var currentYoffset = 0;
        game.board.forEach(function checkLine(line) {
            line = line.split('');
            var currentXoffset = 0;
            line.forEach(function checkCharacter(character) {
                if(character == '#') {
                    ctx.fillStyle = "black";
                    ctx.fillRect(currentXoffset, currentYoffset, graphics.
squareSize, graphics.squareSize);
                }
                currentXoffset += graphics.squareSize;
            });
            currentYoffset += graphics.squareSize;
        });
    },
```

continues

```
    drawSnake: function(ctx) {
        snake.parts.forEach(function drawPart(part) {
            var partXlocation = part.x * graphics.squareSize;
            var partYlocation = part.y * graphics.squareSize;
            ctx.fillStyle = "green";
            ctx.fillRect(partXlocation, partYlocation, graphics.
squareSize, graphics.squareSize);
        });
    },
    drawGame: function () {
        var ctx = graphics.canvas.getContext("2d");
        graphics.drawBoard(ctx);
        graphics.drawSnake(ctx);
    }
};
graphics.drawGame();
```

🐱 Make sure you have used the correct parentheses ((())) and braces (({})).

🐱 Make sure each property in the object except the final one is followed by a comma (,).

🐱 Don't forget the semicolon (;) at the end of the object.

7. Save your file as **snake3.html** and open it in your browser. A green snake will now be displayed on the game board.

Pay attention to your syntax. Don't forget to use the developer tools in your browser if you get stuck.

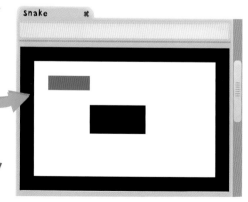

MAKING THE GAME TICK

Now that we have a snake, we need to make it move around the game board. *Noughts and Crosses* in Mission 1 was a turn-based game, so the game state changed only when a player clicked on the screen. *Snake* is a different type of game. The snake has to move on its own without any user input.

In Mission 1, we used a loop to check the rows and columns on the board. The loop ran after each player had clicked on a square. In this mission, we are going to write code that will make our game **tick** by itself using a timer function.

CODE WORDS A **TICK** is a unit of measure for time. It refers to moments of repeated and regular action in a game, normally a loop. The word comes from the "tick" sound a clock makes.

Using the setTimeout function

JavaScript timers, such as the setTimeout function, are very useful for building games. Sometimes we don't want our JavaScript to run the moment the page has loaded, but only after a certain amount of time has passed. To do this, we use the setTimeout function, which looks like this:

setTimeout function   amount of time to call it after

```
setTimeout(function, 1000);
```

function to call

We use setTimeout to call a function after a given interval of time. The unit of time is given in milliseconds; 1,000 milliseconds is equal to one second.

This example shows how you can use setTimeout in a function to make an alert tick. Every 5,000 milliseconds (or 5 seconds), setTimeout will call the tick function and pop up an alert:

```
<script>
    function tick(){
        alert("Lucky Cat Club");
        setTimeout("tick()", 5000);
    }
    tick();
</script>
```

function   call   time

Making the Snake Move

We want to make our snake move a certain number of pixels every 500 milliseconds. This is fast enough to make it look like the snake is moving continuously. We are going to use the setTimeout function like this:

```
game.timer = window.setTimeout("game.tick()", 500);
```

Use setTimeout to make the snake tick. We will add more code to these functions in the next game build.

1. Open your **snake3.html** file. Add an empty tick function to the game object. Also add a variable to keep track of the number of ticks. Remember to use commas in the correct places to separate the properties in the object:

```
var game = {
    tickNumber: 0,
    board: [
        "###############",
        "#             #",
        "#             #",
        "#             #",
        "#             #",
        "#      ####   #",
        "#      ####   #",
        "#             #",
        "#             #",
        "#             #",
        "#             #",
        "###############"
    ],
    tick: function() {
    }
};
```

2. Now add another object called gameControl at the bottom of your <script> block. Add a startGame function that calls the new tick function, like this:

```
graphics.drawGame();
var gameControl = {
    startGame: function () {
        game.tick();
    }
};
gameControl.startGame();
```

3. Now use setTimeout in the tick function within the game object to create a timer and store it in a variable. Use the increment operator (++) to add one to the value stored in the tickNumber variable every time the function is called. Then create a timer that uses setTimeout to call the tick function every 500 milliseconds:

```
tick: function() {
    game.tickNumber++;
    game.timer = window.setTimeout("game.tick()", 500);
}
```

Notice that we are accessing the window object to call setTimeout on the browser window.

4. Add the timer to the game object too, so we can keep track of it. Use null to mean "nothing":

```
var game = {
    tickNumber: 0,
    timer: null,
```

5. The game is now ticking, but the snake still isn't moving! We should move the drawGame function call up the `<script>` block and into the tick function, so that the snake is drawn each time the game ticks:

```
tick: function() {
    game.tickNumber++;
    graphics.drawGame();
    game.timer = window.setTimeout("game.tick()", 500);
}
```

6. We also need to add code that means the snake can move only in empty space on the board, not through the walls or island. Let's start by adding an empty move function to the snake object, like this:

We'll come back to this function in the next Game Build

```
var snake = {
    parts: [
        {x: 4, y: 2},
        {x: 3, y: 2},
        {x: 2, y: 2}
    ],
    facing: "E",
    move: function() {
    }
};
```

(Don't forget to add your comma at the end of the previous property.)

7. Save your code as **snake4.html**. Nothing will happen if you open your browser. We need to learn some new skills before we complete the move function.

MAKING THE SNAKE MOVE

At the moment, we are using an array to draw the snake on-screen. To make it look like the snake is moving across the screen, we have to add or remove items from the array every time the game ticks.

Using Arrays to Create Movement

We can move the snake across the board by adding and removing parts of the array.

> 🐱 **If we add an element to the top of the array, the snake's head moves forward by one square.**
>
> 🐱 **If we remove an element from the bottom of the array, the snake's tail shrinks by one square.**

Coding the snake in this way enables it to turn corners correctly. To add or remove the elements, we need two methods: pop and unshift.

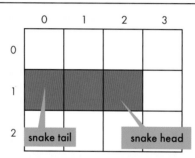

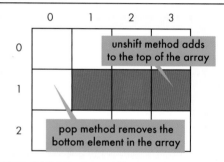

Using unshift

The unshift method adds one or more elements to the beginning of an array and returns the new length of the array each time it's called:

```
.unshift(element);
```

To move the snake's head forward, we use unshift and give the next location for the head as coordinates:

```
snake.parts.unshift({x: 3, y: 1});
```

Using pop

To move the snake's tail along, we use the pop method to remove the last element from the array. This removes the last element and then returns that element as a value.

method

```
snake.parts.pop();
```

94

Pathfinding

We also need to write code that will determine how the snake is going to work out where it should move next. In games, this is known as pathfinding. If we add a function called `nextLocation` to the snake object, we can work out the snake's new direction in the following way:

```
nextLocation: function () {
    var snakeHead = snake.parts[0];          array indexer
    var targetX = snakeHead.x;               x-coordinate
    var targetY = snakeHead.y;               y-coordinate
    targetY = snake.facing == "N" ? targetY-1 : targetY;
    targetY = snake.facing == "S" ? targetY+1 : targetY;    ternary
    targetX = snake.facing == "W" ? targetX-1 : targetX;    operators
    targetX = snake.facing == "E" ? targetX+1 : targetX;
    return {x: targetX, y: targetY};
}
```

Let's look at what we're doing in this function. First we're creating a variable called `snakeHead` that stores the first element in the `parts` array. We're doing this using the array index. The index is the number that corresponds to the place in the array where the value is stored. So the first item in the array—the snake's head—will be zero. By putting zero in brackets ([ ]), we are saying "Get the first (the zero-th) element."

We're then creating two new variables (`targetX` and `targetY`) and storing the current x- and y-coordinates of the snake's head element. Then we use four ternary operators, which we used in Mission 1, to determine the snake's next location, depending on the direction it is currently facing. We're saying:

> 🐱 **If the snake is facing N (north), then the next y-coordinate of the snake is y minus 1.**
> 🐱 **If the snake is facing S (south), then the next y-coordinate of the snake is y plus 1.**
> 🐱 **If the snake is facing W (west), then the next x-coordinate of the snake is x minus 1.**
> 🐱 **If the snake is facing E (east), then the next y-coordinate of the snake is x plus 1.**

Once all the lines of code have run, the `targetX` and `targetY` coordinates will be changed to point to the next location for the snake on the game board.

Did you notice?

When you refer to the first item in the array, you use zero rather than 1, because in computer science everything is zero-indexed. This means it starts from zero rather than 1.

GAME BUILD 5 ▶ MAKING THE SNAKE MOVE

Make the snake move across the board using the unshift and pop methods.

1. Open your **snake4.html** file. Update the move function in the snake object by making the snake move one square from its current position. Use the unshift method to add a new item at the top of the parts array to move its head. Then remove an element from the end of the snake's tail using pop:

```
move: function() {
    var location = {x: 5, y: 2};
    snake.parts.unshift(location);
    snake.parts.pop();
}
```

2. Now we need to make sure that snake.move gets called every time the loop ticks. To do this, we add it to the game.tick function:

```
tick: function() {
    game.tickNumber++;
    snake.move();
    graphics.drawGame();
    game.timer = window.setTimeout("game.tick()", 500);
}
```

3. Save your file as **snake5.html** and open it in your browser. The snake will move one square to the right.

Before:

After:

2

4. We need to work out how to keep the snake from moving by itself. Add an empty function to the snake called nextLocation. Change your move function so it is accessing the nextLocation function, and remove pop for the time being.

```
var snake = {
    parts: [
        {x: 4, y: 2},
        {x: 3, y: 2},
        {x: 2, y: 2}
    ],
    facing: "E",
    nextLocation: function() {
    },
    move: function() {
        var location = snake.nextLocation();
        snake.parts.unshift(location);
        snake.parts.pop();
    }
};
```

5. The nextLocation function needs to determine where the snake is going to move to next. Use the array index to locate the snake's head and then four ternary operators to decide what should happen if the snake is facing north, south, west, or east.

```
nextLocation: function() {
    var snakeHead = snake.parts[0];
    var targetX = snakeHead.x;
    var targetY = snakeHead.y;
    targetY = snake.facing == "N" ? targetY-1 : targetY;
    targetY = snake.facing == "S" ? targetY+1 : targetY;
    targetX = snake.facing == "W" ? targetX-1 : targetX;
    targetX = snake.facing == "E" ? targetX+1 : targetX;
    return {x: targetX, y: targetY};
},
```

continues

6. If you save your code and refresh your browser, you'll see something like this:

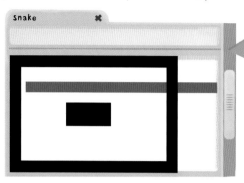

That doesn't look right! The snake keeps growing off the game board. This is because the way we coded the drawing function lets the function keep drawing over itself without first clearing the screen.

7. We need to change the drawGame function to clear the screen on every tick. Let's make a tiny change to it:

```
drawGame: function() {
    var ctx = graphics.canvas.getContext("2d");
    ctx.clearRect(0, 0, graphics.canvas.width, graphics.canvas.height);
    graphics.drawBoard(ctx);
    graphics.drawSnake(ctx);
}
```

By calling this code before drawing the board and snake, we clear the screen as our snake moves.

8. Finally, make the tail move along with the head by adding pop back into the **move** function:

```
move: function() {
    var location = snake.nextLocation();
    snake.parts.unshift(location);
    snake.parts.pop();
}
```

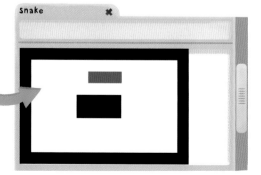

9. Save your code and refresh your browser. Your snake will move across the screen on its own. Now we need to keep it within the walls and control its direction.

CONTROLLING THE SNAKE

We now have code that reacts to the way the snake is facing, but there is no way for the player to move the snake around the board. We're going to have to add input handling, which will let us use the keyboard to control the snake. We need to expand the gameControl object to do things when the player presses certain keys.

eventListeners

In your browser, every time you click, type on the keyboard, or use your mouse, you create an event. You can keep track of, or "listen to," these events by using a method called eventListener. Your browser comes with lots of built-in events:

> abort, beforeinput, blur, click, compositionstart, compositionupdate, compositionend, dblclick, error, focus, focusin, focusout, input, keydown, **keypress**, keyup, load, mousedown, mouseenter, mouseleave, mousemove, mouseout, mouseover, mouseup, resize, scroll, select, unload, wheel

To use the eventListener method, we have to include three pieces of information: the event, the function we want to call, and the use capture. The event we need for our game is keypress.

We want to use an eventListener to call a function every time a key has been pressed. Then we can decide what the key should do to the snake. First look at this example:

```
<script>
    function whenAKeyIsPressed(keyPressed) {
        alert(keyPressed.key);
    }
    window.addEventListener("keypress", whenAKeyIsPressed, false);
</script>
```

eventListener — function — use capture — function — built-in event

Using the eventListener method and the keypress event, we can pop up the value of any key on the keyboard. If you press the C key on the keyboard, this is what the alert will display:

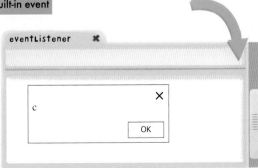

WASD Controls

To control the snake, we need to create some keyboard controls to go with the keypress event. We're going to use WASD controls, which is when you use the W, A, S, and D keys on your keyboard like arrows. The W and S keys control upward and downward movement, while A and D control left and right movement:

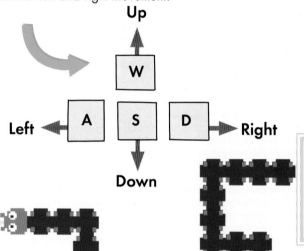

We want to make each WASD key move the snake in a different direction: north, south, east, or west.

Key	Snake direction
W	North
A	West
S	South
D	East

Did you notice?

In gaming, WASD keys are often used instead of the arrow keys because it allows the player to use the mouse with their right hand and the keys with their left.

Using clearTimeout

We also need to be able to stop the game from ticking for a second time once a key has been pressed. Otherwise, every time the game ticks, the snake will get faster. We need to use the opposite function of setTimeout: clearTimeout. This stops a function from being called after a certain amount of time.

```
<script>
    function saberTooth() {
        alert("Research rivals!");
    }                    clearTimeout
    var timeout = window.setTimeout("saberTooth()", 500);
    window.clearTimeout(timeout);
</script>              timer to cancel
```

This example shows that if you call clearTimeout and pass the timer variable as an argument, it will stop the timer.

GAME BUILD 6 ►

Use an eventListener so the player can control the snake's movement with the WASD keys on the keyboard.

1. Open your **snake5.html** file. Add a new function to the gameControl object called processInput. Then, in the startGame function, use an eventListener to tell the browser to call the processInput function every time the keypress event happens:

```
var gameControl = {
    processInput: function(keyPressed) {
    },
    startGame: function() {
        window.addEventListener("keypress", gameControl.processInput, false);
        game.tick();
    }
};
```

2. Now we need to expand the processInput function so something will happen when a WASD key is pressed. We can do this using if statements with the equal to (==) operator to change the target direction once the player presses the key. Use the toLowerCase method to convert the key to lowercase.

```
processInput: function (keyPressed) {
    var key = keyPressed.key.toLowerCase();
    var targetDirection = snake.facing;
    if(key == "w") targetDirection = "N";
    if(key == "a") targetDirection = "W";
    if(key == "s") targetDirection = "S";
    if(key == "d") targetDirection = "E";
    snake.facing = targetDirection;
},
```

Hooray! We can control the snake!

3. Save your code as **snake6.html** and open it in your browser. You can now control the snake using the WASD keys.

4. Did you notice the snake was a little slow to respond to your key presses? That's because it won't move again until the next tick in the game. When you play a game, you want the controls to work the moment you press a button. If we call `game.tick()` after we've pressed the keys, the game will feel more responsive:

```
processInput: function (keyPressed) {
    var key = keyPressed.key.toLowerCase();
    var targetDirection = snake.facing;
    if(key == "w") targetDirection = "N";
    if(key == "a") targetDirection = "W";
    if(key == "s") targetDirection = "S";
    if(key == "d") targetDirection = "E";
    snake.facing = targetDirection;
    game.tick();
},
```

 However, if you save the code and refresh your browser, you'll notice a new bug. Every time the game ticks, it sets up a new timer to tick again in 500 milliseconds. This means that every time we press a key, the game speeds up! We can solve this problem using `clearTimeout`.

5. Modify the `tick` function so that it clears the timer every time it's called. This means that while our game is ticking, it's not going to accidentally try to run a second time because someone presses a direction key.

```
tick: function () {
    window.clearTimeout(game.timer);
    game.tickNumber++;
    snake.move();
    graphics.drawGame();
    game.timer = window.setTimeout("game.tick()", 500);
}
```

6. Save, refresh, and try it out! Your snake should now feel much more responsive.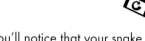

You'll notice that your snake can still move through the walls and island. Let's fix that now.

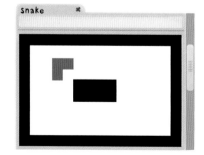

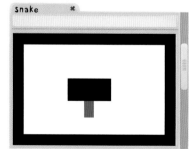

WALLS AND COLLISIONS

The snake can pass through the walls and island of the board because we haven't used collision detection in our game. We need to write code that can use the game board and the snake's location to tell us if the snake has touched a wall or the island.

Collision Detection

Collision detection is code that can tell if two objects have bumped into each other or are on top of each other. We need a new function that determines if space in front of the snake is clear or if there is an obstacle in the way:

```
isEmpty: function(location) {
    var contents = game.board[location.y][location.x];
    return contents == ' ';
}
```

array indexer

space character

We're accessing the board array in our game object. Then we are checking if the space the snake wants to move into is an empty space character and clear of obstacles. By passing the location, we can use the array indexer to first access the y and x locations. We can even simplify our isEmpty function further so we do it all in one line.

```
isEmpty: function(location) {
    return game.board[location.y][location.x] == ' ';
}
```

We can then put the new isEmpty function in the snake.move function as part of an if statement to stop the snake from moving through the walls:

We're also passing the location as an argument so the snake can check if the location is empty before it moves there.

```
move: function () {
    var location = snake.nextLocation();
    if(game.isEmpty(location)) {
        snake.parts.unshift(location);
        snake.parts.pop();
    }
}
```

How can we make the snake collide?

Add collision detection to the game so the snake can't move through the walls.

1. Open your **snake6.html** file. First add a function called `isEmpty` to the game object and pass it the argument `location`. We'll add more code here in a few steps.

```
var game = {
. . .
    tick: function() {
        window.clearTimeout(game.timer);
        game.tickNumber++;
        snake.move();
        graphics.drawGame();
        game.timer = window.setTimeout("game.tick()", 500);
    },
    isEmpty: function(location) {
    }
};
```

2. Now call the `isEmpty` function from the `snake.move` function by adding an if statement:

```
move: function() {
    var location = snake.nextLocation();
    if(game.isEmpty(location)) {
        snake.parts.unshift(location);
        snake.parts.pop();
    }
}
```

3. Make the `isEmpty` function check if the snake is able to pass into an empty space. Use the board array and the array indexer:

```
isEmpty: function(location) {
    var contents = game.board[location.y][location.x];
    return contents == ' ';
}
```

4. We can even simplify our function further so we do it all in one line.

```
isEmpty: function(location) {
    return game.board[location.y][location.x] == ' ';
}
```

5. Save your code as **snake7.html** and open it in your browser. The snake will not be able to pass through walls or the island.

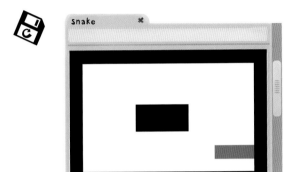

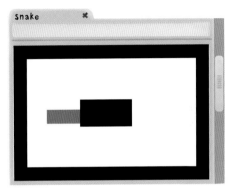

GAME OVER

Now that we've got collision detection up and running, let's make sure that when the snake hits a wall, the game ends and the player is alerted. We can do this using the `isEmpty` function that's already in our code and a new function that

checks if the snake's next location is a wall. The two methods are very similar. Instead of checking for an empty space, we are checking for the hash (#) character, which we used to create the game board's walls and island.

We don't want the game to just stop. We want the player to know it's ended.

GAME BUILD 8 ► GAME OVER

Learn how to end the game when the snake hits a wall.

1. Open your **snake7.html** file. Underneath `isEmpty` in the game object, add a function called `isWall`:

```
isEmpty: function(location) {
    return game.board[location.y][location.x] == ' ';
},
isWall: function(location) {
    return game.board[location.y][location.x] == '#';
}
```

2. We can use the new `isWall` function in the `snake.move` code to work out when we should end the game:

```
move: function () {
    var location = snake.nextLocation();
    if(game.isEmpty(location)) {
        snake.parts.unshift(location);
        snake.parts.pop();
    }
    if(game.isWall(location)) {
        return "gameover";
    }
}
```

3. At the moment, even though we are returning gameover, the game won't actually end until we write the code to stop it. We need to go into the game.tick function and modify the code so that if the snake returns gameover, the timer will stop. We just return from the tick function before the timer gets cued again.

```
tick: function () {
    window.clearTimeout(game.timer);
    game.tickNumber++;
    var result = snake.move();
    if(result == "gameover") {
        alert("Game over!");
        return;
    }
    graphics.drawGame();
}
```

4. Save your code as **snake8.html** and open it in your browser. Now when you move your snake into a wall, the game will end and a game-over alert will pop up.

ADDING A FRUIT

We can now control the snake and end the game, but there's nothing for the player to do other than move around the board. Remember the rules of *Snake*? We're missing fruit from our game. Adding fruit uses the same skills we have learned for coding the snake. All we have to do is add the fruit at the right point in our code and simplify some of our functions. Let's feed our hungry snake!

GAME BUILD 9 ▶ ADDING A FRUIT

Add a fruit to the game board.

1. Open up your **snake8.html** file. Add a fruit by creating a new array underneath the board in the game object. Give the fruit an x and a y property for the top left corner of the board.

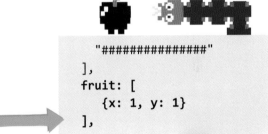

```
      "###############"
    ],
    fruit: [
      {x: 1, y: 1}
    ],
```

2. Now we need to draw the fruit. In the graphics object, add a drawFruit function underneath drawSnake. It will be almost identical:

```
drawFruit: function(ctx) {
    game.fruit.forEach(function(part) {
        var partXlocation = part.x * graphics.squareSize;
        var partYlocation = part.y * graphics.squareSize;
        ctx.fillStyle = "red";
        ctx.fillRect(partXlocation, partYlocation, graphics.
squareSize, graphics.squareSize);
    });
},
```

There are only two differences in the code for our two functions: we're using forEach with game.fruit, and we've changed our fillStyle to red to make our square look like an apple.

continues ▶

3. Call the `drawFruit` function in the `drawGame` function. Add it after the `drawSnake` call.

```
drawGame: function() {
    var ctx = graphics.canvas.getContext("2d");
    ctx.clearRect(0, 0, graphics.canvas.width, graphics.canvas.height);
    graphics.drawBoard(ctx);
    graphics.drawSnake(ctx);
    graphics.drawFruit(ctx);
}
```

> When we have functions that are so similar, we should try to merge them.

4. Finally, combine our `drawSnake` and `drawFruit` functions into a single draw function, passing in the thing we want to draw as an argument. The new draw function will call `forEach` on either `snake.parts` or `game.fruit`, depending on which one is passed as an argument. It will set the `fillStyle` to the third argument we pass.

```
draw: function(ctx, source, color) {
    source.forEach(function(part) {
        var partXlocation = part.x * graphics.squareSize;
        var partYlocation = part.y * graphics.squareSize;
        ctx.fillStyle = color;
        ctx.fillRect(partXlocation, partYlocation, graphics.squareSize,
graphics.squareSize);
    });
},
drawGame: function() {
    var ctx = graphics.canvas.getContext("2d");
    ctx.clearRect(0, 0, graphics.canvas.width, graphics.canvas.height);
    graphics.drawBoard(ctx);
    graphics.draw(ctx, snake.parts, "green");
    graphics.draw(ctx, game.fruit, "red");
}
```

5. Save your code as **snake9.html** and open it in your browser. You should see a fruit in the top left corner of the board.

EATING THE FRUIT

The game now has a fruit, but the snake passes straight through it. We want to use collision detection to know when the snake is touching the fruit. Then we can write code to make the snake eat it. The fruit will disappear from the board, and the snake will grow a square in length. The player will score a point.

Adding Collision Detection to the Fruit

We can use a loop to count through every fruit on the game board, checking it against the position of the snake. The loop will check if the x location of the snake is the same as the x location of the fruit and if the y location of the snake is the same as the y location of the fruit. If the positions are the same, the snake has collided with a fruit and we can return true. Let's look at the loop:

```
for(var fruitNumber = 0; fruitNumber < game.fruit.length; fruitNumber++) {
    var fruit = game.fruit[fruitNumber];
        if(location.x == fruit.x && location.y == fruit.y) {
            return true;
        }
}
```

`loop`

`if statement`

`array indexer`

Using Splice

When the snake eats the fruit, the fruit needs to vanish from the board. We can use the splice method to remove the fruit from the board when the snake detects it. splice adds or removes items from an array and returns the new item. To remove the item, you have to give the item's location in the array using the offset (the x and y numbers we gave to the fruit), counting from the top. So if we want to remove the fruit located at (1_1), we code:

```
if(location.x == fruit.x && location.y == fruit.y) {
    game.fruit.splice(fruitNumber, 1);
    return true;
}
```

`splice method`

`fruit to remove`

`position in array`

Adding to the Score

Every time the snake eats a fruit, we want the player to score a point. To do this, we can use an if statement in the snake.move function to check if the snake and fruit are in the same location. Then the increment operator (++) will add 1 to the score, starting from zero:

```
if(game.isFruit(location)) {
    game.score++;
}
```

increment operator

Making the Snake Grow

Another important thing that needs to happen is that when the snake eats a fruit, it needs to grow a square in length. Remember how unshift moved the head of the snake forward a square and pop removed the tail? To grow the snake when it eats a fruit, we have to unshift the head and not pop the tail. This will make our snake one square bigger. We need to update the if statement to include this:

```
if(game.isFruit(location)) {
    snake.parts.unshift(location);
    game.score++;
}
```

unshift method

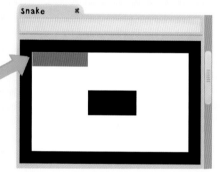

GAME BUILD 10 ► EATING THE FRUIT

Make the snake eat the fruit. The fruit should vanish from the board and the snake should grow in square length.

1. Open your **snake9.html** file. Add another function called isFruit to the game object and set it to return false for the time being.

```
isWall: function(location) {
    return game.board[location.y][location.x] == '#';
},
isFruit: function(location) {
    return false;
}
```

2. The new function is going to work differently from `isEmpty` and `isWall` because instead of checking the board, it's going to use a loop to check the snake's location against the fruit location.

```
isFruit: function(location) {
    for(var fruitNumber = 0; fruitNumber < game.fruit.length; fruitNumber++) {
        var fruit = game.fruit[fruitNumber];
        if(location.x == fruit.x && location.y == fruit.y) {
            return true;
        }
    }
    return false;
}
```

3. We can now use this `isFruit` function to do more interesting things in our `snake.move` code. Add an if statement to pop up an alert if the snake touches a fruit:

```
move: function () {
    var location = snake.nextLocation();
    if(game.isEmpty(location)) {
        snake.parts.unshift(location);
        snake.parts.pop();
    }
    if(game.isWall(location)) {
        return "gameover";
    }
    if(game.isFruit(location)) {
        alert('Fruit');
    }
}
```

Let's feed the snake!

4. Save your file as **snake10.html** and open it in your browser. When the snake runs into a fruit, we're going to see an alert:

continues

5. Now use the `splice` method to remove the fruit from the board once the snake has eaten it:

```
isFruit: function(location) {
    for (var fruitNumber = 0; fruitNumber < game.fruit.length; fruitNumber++){
        var fruit = game.fruit[fruitNumber];
        if(location.x == fruit.x && location.y == fruit.y) {
            game.fruit.splice(fruitNumber, 1);
            return true;
        }
    }
    return false;
},
```

6. We should also change the alert to start counting the score. In the `snake.move` function, replace the alert with the increment operator (`++`) to count the score up from zero, like this:

```
if(game.isFruit(location)) {
    game.score++;
}
```

Now we need to add more fruit!

7. Finally, update the code for eating the fruit so that if the snake and fruit are in the same location, the snake grows one square. Use `unshift`, like this:

```
if(game.isFruit(location)) {
    snake.parts.unshift(location);
    game.score++;
}
```

8. Save your code and refresh your browser. Now when the snake eats the fruit, the fruit will vanish and the snake will grow.

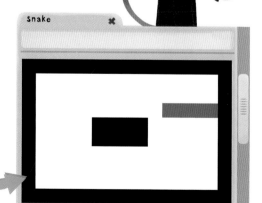

ADDING MORE FRUIT

At the moment, we have only one fruit, which is added at the start of the game. To make the game more challenging, we're going to have to make more fruit appear randomly on the board as the game goes on.

The Remainder Operator

Every ten ticks, we're going to turn a random square on the board into a fruit. To do this, we'll use the remainder operator (%) to code a new if statement in the game.tick function. If the tickNumber divided by 10 is equal to (==) zero, a random fruit will be added to the board. This is because the remainder operator returns zero if our tickNumber is divisible by ten. So every tenth tick, the if statement will run.

remainder operator

```
if(game.tickNumber % 10 == 0) {
    game.addRandomFruit();
}
```

random fruit function

Adding Fruit in Random Places

We need to create a new function to add random fruit to the game. First we need to pick a place to add our fruit. We do this by generating two random numbers. The variable randomY will be a random number between zero and the height of our game board. We'll then pick a randomX, which will be how far across we want to put the fruit on our board.

floor   random

y number

x number

```
addRandomFruit: function() {
    var randomY = Math.floor(Math.random() * game.board.length) + 0;
    var randomX = Math.floor(Math.random() * game.board[randomY].length) + 0;
    var randomLocation = {x: randomX, y: randomY};
    if(game.isEmpty(randomLocation) && !game.isFruit(randomLocation)) {
        game.fruit.push(randomLocation);
    }
},
```

location for fruit

push method

We're using Math.floor and Math.random functions. Calling random generates a random number, and floor makes sure we get only whole numbers (1, 2, 3, 4 and not 1.5, 1.6, 1.7). Store the new randomLocation object in a variable.

Finally, we're using an if statement to check that the random location we have selected is empty, and (&&) there is not (!) already a fruit in that location. If those conditions are true, we can use the push method to draw the fruit in the chosen location. This method adds an item to the end of an array and returns the new length.

GAME BUILD 11 ▶ ADDING RANDOM FRUIT

Add lots of fruit in different places.

1. Open up your **snake10.html** file. Modify the
   `game.tick` function to add fruit every ten ticks:

```
game.tickNumber++;
if(game.tickNumber % 10 == 0) {
    game.addRandomFruit();
}
var result = snake.move();
```

2. Add a new `addRandomFruit` function to the game object, beneath the `tick` function:

```
tick: function () {
    window.clearTimeout(game.timer);
    game.tickNumber++;
    if(game.tickNumber % 10 == 0) {
        game.addRandomFruit();
    }
    var result = snake.move();
    if(result == "gameover") {
        alert("Game over!");
        return;
    }
    graphics.drawGame();
    game.timer = window.setTimeout("game.tick()", 500);
},
addRandomFruit: function() {
},
```

3. We need to make the new function add random fruit to the game. First we're going to have to pick a
   place to add our fruit. Use `floor` and `random` to generate a number for the x and y location. Store
   the new location as an object literal:

```
addRandomFruit: function() {
    var randomY = Math.floor(Math.random() * game.board.length) + 0;
    var randomX = Math.floor(Math.random() * game.board[randomY].length) + 0;
    var randomLocation = {x: randomX, y: randomY};
},
```

4. Once we have the randomLocation, we can add it to the game.fruit array to draw the fruit on-screen, checking that there isn't already a fruit there.

```
addRandomFruit: function() {
    var randomY = Math.floor(Math.random() * game.board.length) + 0;
    var randomX = Math.floor(Math.random() * game.board[randomY].length) + 0;
    var randomLocation = {x: randomX, y: randomY};
    if(game.isEmpty(randomLocation) && !game.isFruit(randomLocation)) {
        game.fruit.push(randomLocation);
    }
},
```

5. If you save your file as **snake11.html** and open it in your browser, a fruit will appear on the board every ten ticks.

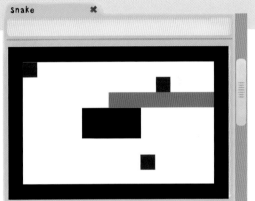

FIXING THE BUGS

Our game works! The player can control the snake, eat fruit, grow longer, and, eventually, crash into a wall and end the game. But there are three bugs left in our code:

- 🐱 The player doesn't know what their score is.

- 🐱 The player can make the snake pass through itself.

- 🐱 Fruit can be randomly drawn on top of the snake.

We need to work out how to fix the bugs in our game.

Let's fix the bugs so the game is ready to play.

1. Open up your **snake11.html** file. Let's start with displaying a score when the game ends. This is easy to fix because we're already counting every time the snake eats a fruit in our game.score variable. All we have to do is make sure we display the value. Change the code in our game.tick function to:

```
if(result == "gameover") {
    alert("Game over! Player scored: " + game.score);
    return;
}
```

2. Also add a score variable to the game object:

```
timer: null,
score: 0,
```

3. Let's fix the second bug and stop the snake from passing through itself. First add a function called isSnake to the end of the game object after isFruit.

```
    }
    isSnake: function(location) {
        return false;
    }
```

4. Then we need to call the new isSnake function in our snake.move function. We can add it to the existing isWall check that ends the game when we crash into a wall. We also need to move the isWall and isSnake checks to the first thing we do in the function. Otherwise, we'll move the snake before we've checked if it should be allowed to move there.

```
move: function () {
    var location = snake.nextLocation();
    if(game.isWall(location)
        || game.isSnake(location)) {
        return "gameover";
    }
    if(game.isEmpty(location)) {
        snake.parts.unshift(location);
        snake.parts.pop();
    }
    if(game.isFruit(location)) {
        snake.parts.unshift(location);
        game.score++;
    }
}
```

5. Finally, we need code to check if the location we pass in is part of the snake at that moment. We can just add a loop to do this, which counts each of our `snake.parts`. This is nearly identical to the code we wrote to check if a fruit was already there. This time we're checking the `snake.parts`.

```
    },
    isSnake: function(location) {
        for(var snakePart = 0; snakePart < snake.parts.length; snakePart++) {
            var part = snake.parts[snakePart];
            if(location.x == part.x && location.y == part.y) {
                return true;
            }
        }
        return false;
    }
```

> Let's beat the bugs and finish the build!

6. Now that we've stopped the snake from being able to pass through itself, there's an interesting new bug. If you press opposite keyboard keys—for example, if the snake is traveling east and you press the A key to make it go west—the snake will eat itself and you'll lose the game instantly!

We should change our input handling in the gameControl object to stop the snake from being able to turn in on itself. All we have to do is check in each of our if statements to see if the snake is facing the exact opposite direction of the key that was pressed.

```
var gameControl = {
    processInput: function(keyPressed) {
        var key = keyPressed.key.toLowerCase();
        var targetDirection = snake.facing;
        if(key == "w" && snake.facing != "S") targetDirection = "N";
        if(key == "a" && snake.facing != "E") targetDirection = "W";
        if(key == "s" && snake.facing != "N") targetDirection = "S";
        if(key == "d" && snake.facing != "W") targetDirection = "E";
        snake.facing = targetDirection;
        game.tick();
    },
```

Now the snake can't turn on the spot!

continues

7. We have one final bug: fruit can be drawn on top of the snake if it's randomly generated under its tail. The simplest way to solve this is to make sure that our snake always gets drawn on the screen after the fruit. Change the last two lines of the drawGame function in the graphics object so the fruit is drawn first.

```
drawGame: function () {
    var ctx = graphics.canvas.getContext("2d");
    ctx.clearRect(0, 0, graphics.canvas.width, graphics.canvas.height);
    graphics.drawBoard(ctx);
    graphics.draw(ctx, game.fruit, "red");
    graphics.draw(ctx, snake.parts, "green");
}
```

With the snake being drawn last, even if we randomly place a fruit under its tail, we won't see it until the snake moves off that square.

8. Save your code as **snake12.html** and open it in your browser. The bugs are fixed!

Hooray! We've done it!

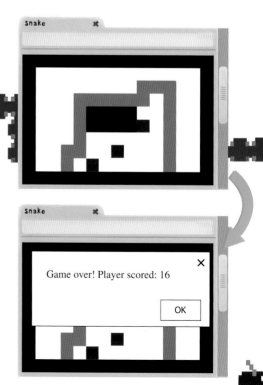

Snake

Snake

Game over! Player scored: 16

OK

SUPER SKILLS

Our game of *Snake* is now finished. How well can you play it? The difficulty of our game comes from how fast the snake moves and how many fruits are on the board at once.

Taking your game further

🐱 Change the layout of the walls and the island on the game board by editing the board array. Change how the hash (#) characters are arranged to get different formations.

🐱 Can you work out how to make the snake move faster?
(Hint: The snake moves at the speed the game ticks.)

🐱 The drawGame function is drawing the walls, snake, and fruit as a series of colored squares. You could change what you pass to graphics.draw to draw parts of the game world in different ways. Can you think of a way to change the color of just the snake's head?

🐱 Can you create multiple levels for your game by creating more than one board array?

Future game builds

Snake is a tick-based puzzle game, with the character moving on every tick of the game. The same skills and techniques are used to make versions of classic games such as *Tetris* and *Pac-Man*, as well as games played today such as *Candy Crush Saga*.

MISSION 2: FINAL CODE

```html
<!DOCTYPE html>
<html>
<head>
    <title>Snake</title>
</head>
<body>
    <canvas id="canvas" width="1024" height="1024"></canvas>
    <script>
    var game = {
        tickNumber: 0,
        timer: null,
        score: 0,
        board: [
            "###############",
            "#             #",
            "#             #",
            "#             #",
            "#     ####    #",
            "#     ####    #",
            "#             #",
            "#             #",
            "#             #",
            "###############"
        ],
        fruit: [
            {x: 1, y: 1}
        ],
        tick: function() {
            window.clearTimeout(game.timer);
            game.tickNumber++;
            if(game.tickNumber % 10 == 0) {
                game.addRandomFruit();
            }
            var result = snake.move();
            if(result == "gameover") {
                alert("Game over! Player scored: " + game.score);
                return;
            }
```

```
            graphics.drawGame();
            game.timer = window.setTimeout("game.tick()", 500);
        },
        addRandomFruit: function() {
            var randomY = Math.floor(Math.random() * game.board.length) + 0
            var randomX = Math.floor(Math.random() * game.board[randomY].length) + 0;
            var randomLocation = {x: randomX, y: randomY};
            if(game.isEmpty(randomLocation) && !game.isFruit(randomLocation)) {
                game.fruit.push(randomLocation);
            }
        },
        isEmpty: function(location) {
            return game.board[location.y][location.x] == ' ';
        },
        isWall: function(location) {
            return game.board[location.y][location.x] == '#';
        },
        isFruit: function(location) {
            for(var fruitNumber = 0; fruitNumber < game.fruit.length; fruitNumber++) {
                var fruit = game.fruit[fruitNumber];
                if(location.x == fruit.x && location.y == fruit.y) {
                    game.fruit.splice(fruitNumber, 1);
                    return true;
                }
            }
            return false;
        },
        isSnake: function(location) {
            for(var snakePart = 0; snakePart < snake.parts.length; snakePart++) {
                var part = snake.parts[snakePart];
                if(location.x == part.x && location.y == part.y) {
                    return true;
                }
            }
            return false;
        }
};
var snake = {
    parts: [
        {x: 4, y: 2},
        {x: 3, y: 2},
        {x: 2, y: 2}
    ],
    facing: "E",
```

continues

```javascript
        nextLocation: function() {
            var snakeHead = snake.parts[0];
            var targetX = snakeHead.x;
            var targetY = snakeHead.y;
            targetY = snake.facing == "N" ? targetY-1 : targetY;
            targetY = snake.facing == "S" ? targetY+1 : targetY;
            targetX = snake.facing == "W" ? targetX-1 : targetX;
            targetX = snake.facing == "E" ? targetX+1 : targetX;
            return {x: targetX, y: targetY};
        },
        move: function() {
            var location = snake.nextLocation();
            if(game.isWall(location)
                || game.isSnake(location)) {
                return "gameover";
            }
            if(game.isEmpty(location)) {
                snake.parts.unshift(location);
                snake.parts.pop();
            }
            if(game.isFruit(location)) {
                snake.parts.unshift(location);
                game.score++;
            }
        }
    };
    var graphics = {
        canvas: document.getElementById("canvas"),
        squareSize: 30,
        drawBoard: function(ctx) {
            var currentYoffset = 0;
            game.board.forEach(function checkLine(line) {
                line = line.split('');
                var currentXoffset = 0;
                line.forEach(function checkCharacter(character) {
                    if(character == '#') {
                        ctx.fillStyle = "black";
                        ctx.fillRect(currentXoffset, currentYoffset, graphics.squareSize,
graphics.squareSize);
                    }
                    currentXoffset += graphics.squareSize;
                });
```

```
                    currentYoffset += graphics.squareSize;
                });
            },
            draw: function(ctx, source, color) {
                source.forEach(function(part) {
                    var partXlocation = part.x * graphics.squareSize;
                    var partYlocation = part.y * graphics.squareSize;
                    ctx.fillStyle = color;
                    ctx.fillRect(partXlocation, partYlocation, graphics.squareSize, graphics.squareSize);
                });
            },
            drawGame: function() {
                var ctx = graphics.canvas.getContext("2d");
                ctx.clearRect(0, 0, graphics.canvas.width, graphics.canvas.height);
                graphics.drawBoard(ctx);
                graphics.draw(ctx, game.fruit, "red");
                graphics.draw(ctx, snake.parts, "green");
            }
        };
        var gameControl = {
            processInput: function(keyPressed) {
                var key = keyPressed.key.toLowerCase();
                var targetDirection = snake.facing;
                if(key == "w" && snake.facing != "S") targetDirection = "N";
                if(key == "a" && snake.facing != "E") targetDirection = "W";
                if(key == "s" && snake.facing != "N") targetDirection = "S";
                if(key == "d" && snake.facing != "W") targetDirection = "E"
                snake.facing = targetDirection;
                game.tick();
            },
            startGame: function () {
                window.addEventListener("keypress", gameControl.processInput, false);
                game.tick();
            }
        };
        gameControl.startGame();
        </script>
    </body>
</html>
```

We're definitely going to beat SaberTooth Studios with this game!

Mission 3

TABLE TENNIS

- CODE A REAL-TIME GAME THAT RUNS ON A 60-FRAMES-PER-SECOND GAME LOOP

- CREATE MORE THAN ONE INSTANCE OF AN OBJECT

- CREATE MORE ADVANCED COLLISION DETECTION

- CODE A SIMPLE PIECE OF ARTIFICIAL INTELLIGENCE (AI) TO CONTROL THE COMPUTER'S PADDLE

Mission Brief

To	me@getcoding.com
CC	Ruby; Markus; Rusty; Scratch
Subject	Mission 3 brief

Hello,

It's so nice to meet you! Thanks for being part of the Lucky Cat Club. I'm Grace. I can't wait for the hackathon. I'm so excited to take on SaberTooth Studios and show them our cool games. Learning to code with the rest of the gang has been so fun, and, of course, we couldn't have gotten this far without you!

I love old arcade games. They are such fun to play. My favorites are the ones based on real sports, like hockey, football, and, best of all, table tennis. I've decided that I want to code a table tennis game for the hackathon. I don't think SaberTooth Studios has ever built a game like it, so it will give us a great chance of winning since it's so different.

My dad says he remembers playing table tennis on an actual arcade machine when he was young. I've been reading about it online. The game was called *Pong,* and it was really popular. Those machines look so old-fashioned now! I'm going to code a new version to play in my browser, but make it look like the original game. The game design is very straightforward — you just need two paddles, a ball, and an area to play on. The ball bounces between the players in a way that's hard to predict.

But the exciting thing is that one of the paddles is controlled by the computer. This means I'm going to have to code some simple AI. How cool is that? I'll be coding a game that can think for itself! Let the battle of the paddles begin!

Purr-fect wishes,

Grace

THE DEVELOPER'S DICTIONARY
Your Guide to Games and Gaming

Table Tennis

From the Developer's Dictionary: Your Guide to Games and Gaming

This entry is about Table Tennis games. For other sports games, see Sports.

Table tennis (also known as Ping-Pong) has been a popular game for more than a hundred years. The aim of the game is to try to hit a small ball back and forth across the table, with a player scoring a point if their opponent fails to return it.

Table tennis has always been a popular idea for a computer game, with *Tennis for Two* being developed as early as 1958. The first commercially successful video-

Table Tennis

Genre:	Sport
Mode:	Two-player
First release:	1972 (as Pong)
Playing time:	1 minute or more (level-dependent)
Skills required:	Quick reactions and observation

game version was called _Pong_, after Ping-Pong, and was developed by <u>Atari</u> in the early 1970s. It became hugely popular in <u>arcades</u>, and Atari quickly became a household name. The game is widely believed to have kick-started the gaming industry, which today is worth billions of dollars.

The original game had simple <u>two-dimensional</u> <u>graphics</u>. The player was able to move the <u>paddle</u> up and down the left side of the screen. The paddle on the right side was controlled by either the computer or another player. The players hit the ball back and forth with the paddles, trying to guess the angle at which the ball will bounce next. Points are scored if a player can't return a shot. In the original arcade game, the player controlled the paddle by turning a knob.

Pong was so popular that many other game manufacturers tried to imitate it. Other versions were also developed, such as _Home Pong_, which you could play using a simple <u>console</u> and a television. _Home Pong_ led to the rise of home video-game consoles as we know them today. In 2012, Atari celebrated _Pong_'s fortieth anniversary by releasing an app so players could play on smartphones or tablets.

TABLE TENNIS

In this mission, we're going to code *Table Tennis*. We're going to build two paddles, a moving ball, and a simple piece of artificial intelligence (AI) to play against. As in the last mission, we will use JavaScript to code a loop to make the game tick and draw the graphics on the screen. For this build, we'll also have to use math to calculate how to make the ball bounce at an unpredictable angle. We're going to work on advanced collision detection, so the players can hit the ball back and forth to each other. Follow the instructions in the Game Builds and you'll soon be ready to play.

The Game Build

Table Tennis is addictive because it's easy to understand but hard to play. It requires quick reactions and good coordination. The game board for our version of *Table Tennis* is very simple and doesn't change as you play. It looks like this:

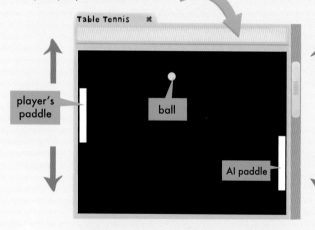

Using the up and down keys on the keyboard, the player can control the paddle on the left side of the screen. The aim is to get the paddle into the correct position so the ball can be bounced back to the other player's paddle, which is controlled by AI. To make the game more of a challenge, we also want to speed up the ball slightly every time it collides with a paddle. If a player misses the ball, the game restarts.

THE GAME BOARD

Because the game board for this game is just a simple black rectangle, we are going to use the <canvas> element and APIs to draw it as we did in Mission 2. We also need to code a function that ticks a speedy 60 times per second to draw the board on-screen.

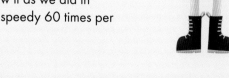

```
<body>
    <canvas id="canvas" width="640" height="480"></canvas>
    <script>
        var canvas = document.getElementById("canvas")
        var ctx = canvas.getContext("2d");
        function tick() {
            draw();
            window.setTimeout("tick()", 1000/60);
        }
        function draw() {
            ctx.fillStyle = "black";
            ctx.fillRect(0, 0, 640, 480);
        }
        tick();
    </script>
</body>
```

canvas

tick function

getContext

timer

draw function

fillStyle

fillRect

The code for the basic structure of the game board will look like this.

This code will draw the game board on-screen.

We're using getContext, fillRect, and fillStyle to code the black rectangle that the game will be played on. We're grouping these APIs into a draw function. We're also coding a tick function that calls the draw function a certain number of times per second. This means that every time the game ticks, the game board will be drawn on-screen.

Making the Game Tick

Let's take a look at the tick function we're using to draw the board on-screen. Using setTimeout, as we did on page 91 for Mission 2, we've created a timer. The timer will enable us to call the code in the draw function 60 times per second. This number, sometimes called "60 frames per second," is often used for drawing games on-screen because it makes the graphics feel smooth when you play. The number of frames per second is fast enough to trick the human eye into seeing the changes in graphics as movement.

JavaScript times everything in milliseconds, so we need to do some math to work out how often we should call the tick function. Because we know we want to update the screen 60 times per second, working out setTimeout is easy.

First, we convert 1 second into milliseconds:

1 second = 1,000 milliseconds

Then we divide our 1,000 milliseconds by 60:

1,000 / 60 = 16.66 milliseconds

129

We want the game to tick every 16.66 milliseconds. JavaScript can perform this calculation for us, so we just use the code:

tick function

```
function tick() {
    draw();
    window.setTimeout("tick()", 1000/60);
}
```

draw function call

timer | function to call | frequency

The game board will be drawn on-screen:

GAME BUILD 1 ▶ THE GAME BOARD

Let's make the board tick 60 times per second.

Build the game board and make it tick using setTimeout.

1. Start a new HTML file called **tennis1.html**. Code the basic structure of your page, using the <canvas> element, like this:

```html
<!DOCTYPE html>
<html>
    <head>
        <title>Table Tennis</title>
    </head>
    <body>
        <canvas id="canvas" width="640" height="480"></canvas>
        <script>
        </script>
    </body>
</html>
```

2. Locate the <canvas> using getElementById as we did on page 71. Create a variable called canvas, and assign a reference to the <canvas> tag by using getElementById to search for the tag's id attribute. Then use getContext to put our 2-D rendering into a variable called ctx. This will let us draw shapes on the screen, just as we did in the last mission. Your code will look like this:

130

```
<canvas id="canvas" width="640" height="480"></canvas>
<script>
    var canvas = document.getElementById("canvas");
    var ctx = canvas.getContext("2d");
</script>
```

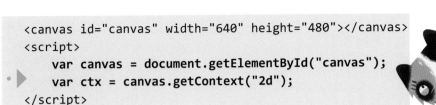

3. Now use setTimeout to create a timer. Code a tick function that calls itself 60 times a second:

```
<script>
    var canvas = document.getElementById("canvas");
    var ctx = canvas.getContext("2d");
    function tick() {
        window.setTimeout("tick()", 1000/60);
    }
    tick();
</script>
```

Notice that we're using setTimeout inside the tick function, before the function call. We're doing this because we want the game to repeatedly tick.

4. At the moment, the game is just an empty screen, so add a draw function to the code and call it from inside the tick function:

```
function tick() {
    draw();
    window.setTimeout("tick()", 1000/60);
}
function draw() {
}
tick();
```

5. Use fillRect to draw the game board. Set the fillStyle to black, and fill a square 640 pixels wide and 480 pixels high—the width and height of the <canvas>:

```
function draw () {
    ctx.fillStyle = "black";
    ctx.fillRect(0, 0, 640, 480);
}
```

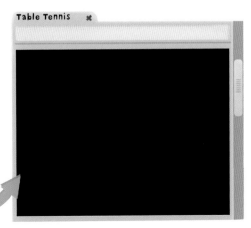

Table Tennis ✖

6. Save your code and open it in your browser. You'll see a black rectangle. This is the game board. Now we can add the paddles and the ball.

CREATING THE PADDLES

There are two paddles in *Table Tennis*, one controlled by the player and one controlled by the computer. The paddles are positioned on the left and right sides of the screen. Now that we have the game board, we need to code the paddles and store data associated with each of them: where they are on the screen and whether they are moving or not. Later in the game, we will work out how to make the player control one paddle and AI control the other.

Defining Objects with Functions

We've looked at JavaScript objects in Mission 2 and seen how we group related functions and variables into a namespace. So far we've been defining objects using object literals, where we've typed out the properties each time. But in JavaScript, we can also use a function to create an object, and then use the new operator to create more than one instance of that object in our code. Objects share functions, but not variables. Let's have a look at an example where we are using a function to define an object:

> This will save us time and space in our code.

```
<script>
    function skateboard(style, owner) {
        this.style = style;
        this.owner = owner;
        this.alertOwner = function() {
            alert(this.owner);
        };
    }
    var skateboard1 = new skateboard("red", "Markus");
    var skateboard2 = new skateboard("green", "Ruby");
    skateboard1.alertOwner();
    skateboard2.alertOwner();
</script>
```

function

new operator

new object

new object

In this example, we've created a function that will define a new skateboard object. The object takes two arguments: style and owner. When this function is called, the this keyword will enable us to access the two arguments passed to the function. Information about the style and owner will be stored inside the skateboard object, but these pieces of information can be different. The skateboard function acts as a template. It means we can now create new skateboard objects elsewhere in our code. These are known as object instances.

To create the new instances of the skateboard object, we use the new operator. We're storing the new instances in two variables: skateboard1 and skateboard2. Did you notice that for each skateboard object, we're passing different arguments to the skateboard function? Those pieces of data are being stored inside the two different object instances. Finally, we can call the alert function on each instance, to alert the owner of each skateboard. Even though we've created each object with the same function, the data stored inside them is different and a new alert will pop up for each object.

```
Objects                    ✱
                    ┌─────────────────┐  ✕
                    │                 │
                    │  Markus         │
                    │          ┌────┐ │
                    │          │ OK │ │
                    │          └────┘ │
                    └─────────────────┘
```

```
Objects              ✱
        ┌─────────────────┐  ✕
        │                 │
        │  Ruby           │
        │          ┌────┐ │
        │          │ OK │ │
        │          └────┘ │
        └─────────────────┘
```

Coding the Paddles

> See how the x-coordinate is different for the top left corner of each paddle.

In our game, we can use object instances to code two paddles that share the same move functions but are located in different places on the board. This is because the location variables inside the paddle objects are stored in each individual instance of the object. Building the game in this way saves time, as it means we only have to code the paddle and its functions once. We can then create two instances of that object: one for the player and one that the computer will control with AI.

The paddle function needs to contain four arguments: the x- and y-coordinates for the top left corner of the paddle, along with the width and height we want to render it:

```
function paddle(x, y, width, height) {
    this.x = x;
    this.y = y;
    this.width = width;
    this.height = height;
}
var player = new paddle(5, 200, 25, 100);
var ai = new paddle(610, 200, 25, 100);
```

paddle function
player paddle
x-coordinate
y-coordinate
AI paddle
width
height

When we create two instances of the `paddle` object, we need to pass different x locations using pixels. We want the top left corner of the player's paddle to be 5 pixels from the left of the screen and 200 pixels down. We also want both paddles to be 25 pixels wide and 100 pixels high.

The AI paddle needs to be positioned on the right side of the screen, so we need to do some math. Remember we said our game was 640 pixels wide by 480 pixels high? In order to work out where we need to put the top left corner of our right-hand paddle, we do the following calculation:

[Total width of the screen]	minus	[Width of the paddle]	minus	[5 pixel gap]	=	[Position]
640	–	25	–	5	=	610

All we have to do now is code a new function that will draw the paddle using the same <canvas> APIs that we used to draw the game board. The two paddles will then be rendered on-screen.

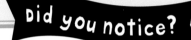

Did you notice?

Remember that in computer science, the x-coordinate is across the screen and the y-coordinate is down the screen.

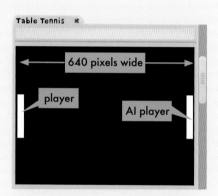

Table Tennis

640 pixels wide

player

AI player

GAME BUILD 2 ▶ CREATING THE PADDLES

Code the paddles using a function to define two object instances.

1. Open your **tennis1.html** file. Create a function that defines the `paddle` object. The function needs four arguments: the x and y location for the top left corner of each paddle, as well as its width and height:

```
var canvas = document.getElementById("canvas");
var ctx = canvas.getContext("2d");
function paddle(x, y, width, height) {
    this.x = x;
    this.y = y;
    this.width = width;
    this.height = height;
}
```

2. Use the new operator to create the player and the ai object instances. Pass the following arguments so the paddles are positioned to the left and right and are the same shape and size:

```
        this.height = height;
    }
var player = new paddle(5, 200, 25, 100);
var ai = new paddle(610, 200, 25, 100);
```

3. We're going to add a new `renderPaddle` function underneath the `draw` function, which takes a single argument: the paddle you want to draw on the screen. All we're doing is using the `fillRect` <canvas> API again. Instead of giving each location, we're going to use the x, y, width, and height properties of the paddle to draw them in the correct location on the screen.

```
function renderPaddle(paddle) {
    ctx.fillStyle = "white";
    ctx.fillRect(paddle.x, paddle.y, paddle.width, paddle.height);
}
tick();
```

4. Once we've added `renderPaddle`, we need to call it from the `draw` function for each player:

The function will use the different values stored in our objects so two different paddles will be drawn in the correct position on the screen.

```
function draw() {
    ctx.fillStyle = "black";
    ctx.fillRect(0, 0, 640, 480);
    renderPaddle(player);
    renderPaddle(ai);
}
```

5. Save your file as **tennis2.html** and open it in your browser. You will now see the paddles on the game board.

Now let's add the ball!

ADDING A MOVING BALL

Like the paddles, the ball in *Table Tennis* has some important data associated with it: its x and y location, its radius (the distance from the center of the ball to the edge), and its speed. We need to create a ball object and use some new <canvas> APIs to render it.

Drawing the Ball

Because there is only one ball in the game, we can create it as an object literal. Our ball object needs the following properties:

ball object — x location — y location — radius — speed across — speed downward

```
var ball = { x: 320, y: 240, radius: 3, xSpeed: 2, ySpeed: 0 };
```

We're going to plot the center of the ball using an x value of 320 pixels and a y value of 240 pixels, which is roughly the middle of our game board. The radius of the ball is 3 pixels. This means the ball will be 3 pixels all the way around. The speed properties will make the ball move across or up and down the screen. To draw the ball on-screen, we need a new function:

Using the <canvas> APIs beginPath, arc, and fill, we're drawing a white

```
function renderBall(ball) {
    ctx.beginPath();            beginPath API          calculation to draw a round ball
    ctx.arc(ball.x, ball.y, ball.radius, 0, 2 * Math.PI, false);
    ctx.fillStyle = "white";
    ctx.fill();
}                               fill API
```

arc API

circle on the game board. We're passing the properties stored in the ball object to arc, along with a math calculation to make it round. We're also setting the fillStyle to white so we can see the ball.

Creating Speed

To make the ball move, we want to add the speed of the ball object to the current x- and y-coordinates every time the game ticks. We need to code a new updateGame function that uses the addition assignment operator (+=) to add the value to the variables. This will force the ball to move.

```
function updateGame() {
    ball.x += ball.xSpeed;
    ball.y += ball.ySpeed;
}
```

current coordinate — addition assignment operator — speed

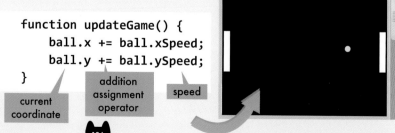

Table Tennis

GAME BUILD 3 ▶ ADDING A MOVING BALL

Use the new <canvas> APIs to add the ball to the board. Then make it move.

1. Open up your saved **tennis2.html** file. Create a ball object literal underneath the paddles. We're going to use an x value of 320 pixels, a y value of 240 pixels, and a radius of 3 pixels:

```
var player = new paddle(5, 200, 25, 100);
var ai = new paddle(610, 200, 25, 100);
var ball = { x: 320, y: 240, radius: 3 };
```

2. We need a renderBall function that uses the new beginPath and arc <canvas> APIs. Add it underneath the renderPaddle function and set the fillStyle to white so we can see the ball on the black board:

```
    ctx.fillRect(paddle.x, paddle.y, paddle.width, paddle.height);
}
function renderBall(ball) {
    ctx.beginPath();
    ctx.arc(ball.x, ball.y, ball.radius, 0, 2 * Math.PI, false);
    ctx.fillStyle = "white";
    ctx.fill();
}
tick();
```

3. Add a call to the new renderBall function in the existing draw function. This time we're passing the ball object as our argument:

```
function draw() {
    ctx.fillStyle = "black";
    ctx.fillRect(0, 0, 640, 480);
    renderPaddle(player);
    renderPaddle(ai);
    renderBall(ball);
}
```

This is how we built the snake in Mission 2!

continues ➡

4. We've got all the ball elements rendering on-screen, but nothing is happening in our game yet. We need to add some movement to the ball. Add an empty function that updates the game. Call it on every tick, before the game is drawn on-screen:

```
function tick() {
    updateGame();
    draw();
    window.setTimeout("tick()", 1000/60);
}
function updateGame() {
}
```

5. To move the ball, we're going to have to give it a speed. Add the xSpeed and ySpeed attributes to the ball object:

```
var ball = { x: 320, y: 240, radius: 3, xSpeed: 2, ySpeed: 0 };
```

6. Now make the ball move. Every time the game ticks, add the ball speed to the current x- and y-coordinates. This will force the ball to move.

```
function updateGame() {
    ball.x += ball.xSpeed;
    ball.y += ball.ySpeed;
}
```

7. Save your file as **tennis3.html** and open it in your browser. Watch as your ball moves across the screen.

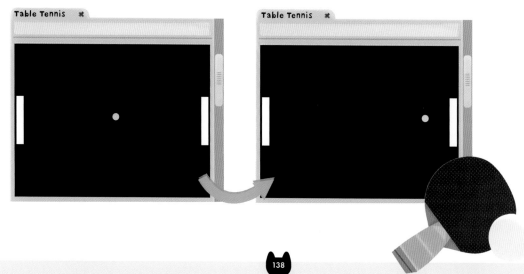

ADDING COLLISION DETECTION

Did you see what just happened? There is no code to check if any of the game elements are bumping into each other. The ball passes through the AI paddle and vanishes from the game. To stop the ball from disappearing off the screen, we need to add collision detection to the paddle object.

Stopping the Ball

To stop the ball, we need to work out its position on the board and the exact moment it touches the paddles. The easiest way to do this is to check whether the ball's x-coordinate is between the right and left wall of each paddle. If it is, the ball has gone too far and needs to stop.

For both instances of the paddle, the x-coordinate of the left wall is the same as the x-coordinate of the paddle, which we coded in

Game Build 2. The x-coordinate of the right wall is the x-coordinate of the paddle **plus** the width of the paddle. We can store the values for the left and right walls in two variables and then use an if statement to decide if the ball should stop.

If the ball's x position is between those two values, we return true to stop the ball. This is our collision detection code. Otherwise, we return false and the ball keeps moving.

```
this.hasCollidedWith = function(ball) {
    var paddleLeftWall = this.x;
    var paddleRightWall = this.x + this.width;
    if(ball.x > paddleLeftWall && ball.x < paddleRightWall) {
        return true;
    }
    return false;
};
```

left side of the paddle

right side of the paddle

greater than operator

and operator

less than operator

CHANGING THE BALL'S DIRECTION

Now that we've stopped the ball, we want to change its direction so it moves back across the board to the other paddle. We need to add code that will reverse the ball's direction. We have to add two new methods: reverseX and reverseY. ReverseX will change the way the ball moves across the screen; reverseY will change the way it moves up or down the screen.

First we use an if statement to check if either of the paddles has collided with the ball:

```
if(player.hasCollidedWith(ball) || ai.hasCollidedWith(ball)) {
    ball.reverseX();
}
```

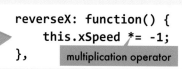

reverse direction function | player's paddle | or operator | AI paddle

If either of the paddles has collided with the ball, we'll then call the new method (in this instance reverseX) to change the direction of the ball on the screen.

We also need some calculations to make the ball change direction in the right way. The calculation we need to add to the ball object for both the x and y speeds is this:

```
reverseX: function() {
    this.xSpeed *= -1;
},
```

multiplication operator

CODE WORDS To **INVERT** means to make the opposite. To invert a positive number means to make it a negative number.

By multiplying (*=) the ball's speed by − 1, we **invert** the number. So if the ball has a speed of 1 and we multiply it by − 1, the speed becomes − 1.

This means that when we next move the ball, instead of adding to the x- or y-coordinate, we're subtracting from it, moving the ball in the opposite direction across the screen.

GAME BUILD 4 ▶ ADDING COLLISION DETECTION

Add collision detection to make the ball move between the two paddles.

1. Open up your saved **tennis3.html** file. Add an empty hasCollidedWith function to the paddle object and pass it the ball as an argument:

```
function paddle(x, y, width, height) {
    this.x = x;
    this.y = y;
    this.width = width;
    this.height = height;
    this.hasCollidedWith = function(ball) {
    };
}
```

Make sure your syntax is correct.

2. Add code to the new `hasCollidedWith` function. Store the left and right walls of the paddle in variables and use an if statement to check if the ball has passed through them:

```
this.hasCollidedWith = function(ball) {
    var paddleLeftWall = this.x;
    var paddleRightWall = this.x + this.width;
    if(ball.x > paddleLeftWall && ball.x < paddleRightWall) {
        return true;
    }
    return false;
};
```

3. Add an if statement to the `updateGame` function that checks if the ball has collided with either of the paddles and reverses its x direction:

```
function updateGame() {
    ball.x += ball.xSpeed;
    ball.y += ball.ySpeed;
    if(player.hasCollidedWith(ball) || ai.hasCollidedWith(ball)) {
        ball.reverseX();
    }
}
```

4. Now make the ball change direction by reversing it. Expand the ball object from this:

```
var ball = { x: 320, y: 240, radius: 3, xSpeed: 2, ySpeed: 0 };
```

to this:

Don't forget the browser developer tools if you get stuck!

```
var ball = {
    x: 320, y: 240, radius: 3, xSpeed: 2, ySpeed: 0,
    reverseX: function() {
        this.xSpeed *= -1;
    },
    reverseY: function() {
        this.ySpeed *= -1;
    }
};
```

continues

5. We should also add some code to make sure the collision detection triggers only when the ball is between the top and bottom of the paddles. We're doing this in the same way we check for the left and right paddle walls, only now we are checking the y-coordinates. Expand the if statement to the following:

```
this.hasCollidedWith = function(ball) {
    var paddleLeftWall = this.x;
    var paddleRightWall = this.x + this.width;
    var paddleTopWall = this.y;
    var paddleBottomWall = this.y + this.height;
    if(ball.x > paddleLeftWall
        && ball.x < paddleRightWall
        && ball.y > paddleTopWall
        && ball.y < paddleBottomWall) {
        return true;
    }
    return false;
};
```

6. Save your file as **tennis4.html** and open it in your browser. Watch the ball move backward and forward between the two paddles.

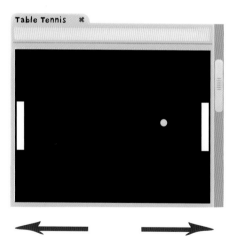

Now let's make those paddles move!

142

CONTROLLING THE PLAYER'S PADDLE

Now that we've got the ball moving, we need to find a way for the player to control the left paddle. When they press the up or down arrow on the keyboard, we want the paddle to move. We're going to use the keypress eventListener as we did in Mission 2. However, instead of processing an input when the key is pressed down, we want the code to keep track of when a key is held down and released.

Bracket Notation

To track when keys are held down, we need to use two new eventListeners: keydown and keyup. When the browser triggers a keydown event, we want to store it in a new heldDown object.

Bracket notation is a quick way to add extra data to an object after you've defined it. We add the data to the object literal using brackets ([]). Once you've defined an object literal, you can add properties to it like this:

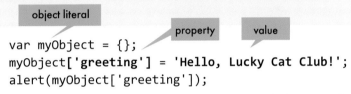

```
var myObject = {};
myObject['greeting'] = 'Hello, Lucky Cat Club!';
alert(myObject['greeting']);
```

Here, we're using brackets to add a new property called greeting to the object. We're setting the value of the property to a string of text.

We can then use the delete keyword to remove the property from the object by its name:

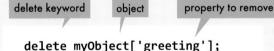

```
delete myObject['greeting'];
alert(myObject['greeting']);
```

If we ran the alert again after using delete, it would return undefined, since the property would have been removed.

Storing the keyCodes

The numbers assigned to each key on a keyboard are known as keyCodes. They give us a way to work out which key a player has pressed. They are especially useful for keys that don't have numbers or letters on them.

We want to use the up and down arrows on the keyboard to control the paddle. To do this, we create an empty heldDown object. We can then add the keydown event and set its keyCode value to the heldDown object. We're going to set our property value to true so that our heldDown object will keep track of every key that is held down. If the keyCode matches the keyCode for the up and down arrows, the paddle will move continuously for as long as the key is held down. We also need to add an eventListener to the keyup event (when we remove our finger), deleting our key from the heldDown object.

empty object · event listener · event · built-in argument · keyword · object · keyCode property

```
var heldDown = {};
window.addEventListener("keydown", function(keyInfo) { heldDown[event.keyCode] = true; }, false);
window.addEventListener("keyup", function(keyInfo) { delete heldDown[event.keyCode]; }, false);
```

Using keyCodes to Create Movement

We can use the keyCode values to make the paddle move:

We want to add a new move function to the paddle object. Depending on the key pressed, we need to change the y property. To move our paddle downward, we need to add pixels to its y property. To move our paddle upward, we need to subtract pixels from its y property:

🐱 The down arrow on your keyboard has the keyCode 40.

🐱 The up arrow on your keyboard has the keyCode 38.

```
this.move = function(keyCode) {
    var nextY = this.y;
    if(keyCode == 40) {
        nextY += 5;
    } else if(keyCode == 38) {
        nextY += -5;
    }
    this.y = nextY;
};
```

keyCode property · down arrow keyCode · pixels to add · up arrow keyCode · pixels to subtract · new paddle position

First we're making a copy of the current y property by creating a variable called nextY and setting its value to the current value of y. Now, if our keyCode is 40 (the down arrow), we're adding 5 pixels to the nextY. Else, if our keyCode is 38 (the up arrow), we're subtracting 5 pixels from the nextY. Finally, we're setting the y value to the value from nextY. The paddle will now move!

Keeping the Paddle on the Game Board

Now that we can move our paddle, we have a new problem. If we keep pressing the up or down key, we can make the paddle go through the floor or ceiling of the game board. Luckily, it's easy to stop this from happening. In the move function, before we set this.y to the value of nextY, we can make sure that our nextY value isn't less than zero pixels (the ceiling of our game) or greater than 480 pixels (the total height of our game). This code overrides our nextY value if it drops below zero or gets bigger than 480:

```
this.move = function(keyCode) {
    var nextY = this.y;
    if(keyCode == 40) {
        nextY += 5;
    } else if (keyCode == 38) {
        nextY += -5;
    }
    nextY = nextY < 0 ? 0 : nextY;
    nextY = nextY + this.height > 480 ? 480 - this.height : nextY;
    this.y = nextY;
};
```

calculation for the top of the board

greater than operator

calculation for the bottom of the board

The first new line is easy to understand. If nextY is less than zero, set nextY to zero. Otherwise, set nextY to its current value.

The second line is a little more complicated because we need to make sure that the bottom edge of the paddle doesn't move past the bottom of our game board. We can calculate the pixel location of the bottom of the paddle by adding nextY to this.height (the height of the paddle). So in our second line, we're checking if nextY plus this.height is greater than 480. If it is greater than (>) 480, then the bottom of the paddle is outside the board, so we're setting the nextY to the value of 480 minus this.height. This is the maximum value that nextY is allowed to be. Otherwise, if nextY + this.height is less than 480, we're leaving the value of nextY as its current value. Now the player's paddle can't pass through the top or bottom of the screen.

This is a tricky calculation!

GAME BUILD 5 ► CONTROLLING THE PLAYER'S PADDLE

Add keyCode controls so the player can move the paddle using the up and down arrows.

1. Open your saved **tennis4.html** file. Toward the end of your `<script>` block, add a new empty heldDown object to store the keys that are currently being pressed down:

```
var heldDown = {};
tick();
```

2. After the new object, add the first eventListener, keydown, using bracket notation. Set the value to true:

```
var heldDown = {};
window.addEventListener("keydown", function(keyInfo) { heldDown[event.keyCode] = true; }, false);
tick();
```

3. We also need to add an eventListener to the keyup event, deleting the key from the heldDown object. Now every time we hold a key down, we'll set true in the heldDown object. When we remove our finger, the keyCode and true value will be removed:

```
var heldDown = {};
window.addEventListener("keydown", function(keyInfo) { heldDown[event.keyCode] = true; }, false);
window.addEventListener("keyup", function(keyInfo) { delete heldDown[event.keyCode]; }, false);
tick();
```

Now it's starting to look like a game!

4. We want the player's paddle on the left side to respond to the keys currently held down. Add a new move function to the paddle object:

```javascript
function paddle (x, y, width, height) {
    this.x = x;
    this.y = y;
    this.width = width;
    this.height = height;
    this.hasCollidedWith = function(ball) {
        var paddleLeftWall = this.x;
        var paddleRightWall = this.x + this.width;
        var paddleTopWall = this.y;
        var paddleBottomWall = this.y + this.height;
        if(ball.x > paddleLeftWall
            && ball.x < paddleRightWall
            && ball.y > paddleTopWall
            && ball.y < paddleBottomWall) {
                return true;
        }
        return false;
    };
    this.move = function() {
    };
}
```

5. Now edit the updateGame function to process the inputs we're storing in the heldDown object. Add a for loop, to loop through every key that is currently held down. Call the move function we just added on the player object. (Remember: our player is just an instance of our paddle object.) Now whenever a key is held down, the player paddle will move.

```javascript
function updateGame() {
    ball.x += ball.xSpeed;
    ball.y += ball.ySpeed;
    var collidedWithPlayer = player.hasCollidedWith(ball);
    var collidedWithAi = ai.hasCollidedWith(ball);
    if(collidedWithPlayer || collidedWithAi) {
        ball.reverseX();
    }
    for(var keyCode in heldDown) {
        player.move(keyCode);
    }
}
function draw() {
```

continues

6. Now add the if and else if statements to the move function in the `paddle` object that will change the paddle's y property, depending on which key is held down:

```
this.move = function(keyCode) {
    var nextY = this.y;
    if(keyCode == 40) {
        nextY += 5;
    } else if(keyCode == 38) {
        nextY += -5;
    }
    this.y = nextY;
};
```

 Save your code as **tennis5.html** and open it in your browser. When you press the up and down keys, your paddle will move. But it will pass through the top and bottom of the board!

7. Let's add the code that will keep the paddle on the game board:

```
this.move = function(keyCode) {
    var nextY = this.y;
    if(keyCode == 40) {
        nextY += 5;
    } else if (keyCode == 38) {
        nextY += -5;
    }
    nextY = nextY < 0 ? 0 : nextY;
    nextY = nextY + this.height > 480 ? 480 - this.height : nextY;
    this.y = nextY;
};
```

> How can we make the game more fun?

 Save your file and refresh your browser. Now the player's paddle can't pass through the top or bottom of the screen.

148

MAKING THE BALL BOUNCE

We can now move the player's paddle and hit the ball back to the AI paddle. But the ball bounces off the paddle in a straight line, which makes the game very predictable and not that fun to play. Let's work out how to make the ball speed up when it collides with the other paddle.

Keeping Track of the Speed

To change the ball's speed, we need to introduce a new property into our paddle object called speedModifier. This variable will keep track of how much the ball speeds up when it collides with the paddle. We will begin by setting it to zero:

```
this.speedModifier = 0;
```

We then need to set the speedModifier in the move function so that when the keys are pressed, the paddles speed up by 1.5 pixels per game tick to keep pace with the ball:

Time to add some bounce!

```
this.move = function(keyCode) {
    var nextY = this.y;
    if(keyCode == 40) {
        nextY += 5;
        this.speedModifier = 1.5;          pixels to speed up by
    } else if(keyCode == 38) {
        nextY += -5;
        this.speedModifier = 1.5;
    } else {
        this.speedModifier = 0;
    }
    nextY = nextY < 0 ? 0 : nextY;
    nextY = nextY + this.height > 480 ? 480 - this.height : nextY;
    this.y = nextY;
};
```

The else statement at the end makes sure that the speedModifier is reset to zero if someone is holding down any other keyboard keys. Now that we're keeping track of how much to speed up the ball, we need to make the ball a little bit smarter.

Changing the Speed across the Board

Now let's write code to change the speed the ball is traveling across the board: the ball's xSpeed. When the ball is traveling toward the right side of the screen, the xSpeed is a positive number. When it's traveling to the left, the xSpeed will be negative:

+ Positive number

Negative number

We need to make sure that the amount we modify the speed matches the direction the ball is traveling in:

```
modification = this.xSpeed < 0 ? modification * -1 : modification;
var nextValue = this.xSpeed + modification;
```

We're using a ternary operator here. When the current xSpeed of the ball is less than (<) zero (the ball is traveling toward the left), we need to multiply (*) the modification by – 1 so it is also a negative number.

Then we simply calculate our nextValue (our new speed) by adding the xSpeed and our modification together. All we need to do after that is set this.xSpeed of our ball to our new speed.

Changing the Speed up and down the Board

We also need to modify the way the ball travels up and down: the ySpeed. Adding bounce to the ball is easy—we're going to do exactly the same thing we did to make the ball speed up. But instead of changing the this.xSpeed property (the horizontal, or left-to-right, speed of the ball), we'll change the this.ySpeed value (the vertical, or up-and-down, speed of the ball) by adding the modified speed to it.

Controlling the Speed

We also need to make sure the ball doesn't speed up too much. We're going to do this by making sure the nextValue is never bigger than 9 pixels of extra speed per game tick. We're going to use a built-in function that will give us the absolute value of a number:

```
nextValue = Math.abs(nextValue) > 9 ? 9 : nextValue;
```

absolute value function

This means that if our nextValue is a negative number, it will return the number without the minus. We're going to check if the total nextValue modification is greater than (>) 9, and if it is, we'll just set it to 9, our maximum speed value. If the nextValue is a negative number, then the maximum speed will be set to – 9.

GAME BUILD 6 ► MAKING THE BALL BOUNCE

Let's make the ball bounce and speed up so the game is harder to play.

1. Open your saved **tennis5.html** file. Add the `speedModifier` property below the `this.height` property in the `paddle` object. Set it to zero like this:

```
function paddle(x, y, width, height) {
    this.x = x;
    this.y = y;
    this.width = width;
    this.height = height;
    this.speedModifier = 0;
    this.hasCollidedWith = function(ball) {
```

2. Now add the `speedModifier` property to the move function. Set it to 1.5 pixels per tick. Add an else statement that will reset the `speedModifier` if any key other than the up or down arrow is pressed:

```
this.move = function(keyCode) {
    var nextY = this.y;
    if(keyCode == 40) {
        nextY += 5;
        this.speedModifier = 1.5;
    } else if(keyCode == 38) {
        nextY += -5;
        this.speedModifier = 1.5;
    } else {
        this.speedModifier = 0;
    }
    nextY = nextY < 0 ? 0 : nextY;
    nextY = nextY + this.height > 480 ? 480 - this.height : nextY;
    this.y = nextY;
};
```

continues ➤

Don't forget to use commas in the correct places.

3. We're going to add three new functions to the ball. Let's start with a new isBouncing function that will check that the ball's speed is not zero. If the ball has a ySpeed that isn't zero, we know the ball is bouncing up or down on the game board. Then code two empty speed functions: modifyXSpeedBy and modifyYSpeedBy.

```javascript
        reverseY: function() {
            this.ySpeed *= -1;
        },
        isBouncing: function() {
            return ball.ySpeed != 0;
        },
        modifyXSpeedBy: function(modification) {
        },
        modifyYSpeedBy: function(modification) {
        }
    };
```

4. Then use a ternary operator to change the xSpeed of the ball as it travels across the screen. Also add a check to stop the ball from going too fast:

```javascript
modifyXSpeedBy: function(modification) {
    modification = this.xSpeed < 0 ? modification * -1 : modification;
    var nextValue = this.xSpeed + modification;
    nextValue = Math.abs(nextValue) > 9 ? 9 : nextValue;
    this.xSpeed = nextValue;
},
```

5. Finally, add code to modify the ball's up-and-down speed:

```javascript
modifyYSpeedBy: function(modification) {
    modification = this.ySpeed < 0 ? modification * -1 : modification;
    this.ySpeed += modification;
}
```

 Save your code as **tennis6.html** and open it in your browser. Your game will be unchanged at this point because we still need to call our new functions.

FINISHING THE BALL

Now that we have coded functions that speed our ball up, we need to make sure they get called at the right points in the game. We also need a way for the game to restart if the player misses a shot.

Implementing the Speed Change

We need to call `modifyXSpeedBy` in the `updateGame` function. We want to speed the ball up only slightly, so we add 0.25 pixels per tick, to make it a quarter faster than it currently is.

```
ball.modifyXSpeedBy(0.25);
```

Bouncing off the Sides

We also want the ball to bounce off the sides of the board. We can simply add a check to our `updateGame` method to make sure that if the ball's y position goes below zero pixels (through the top of our game) or above 480 pixels (through the bottom), we reverse the direction the ball is bouncing, using the `reverseY` function we wrote earlier:

less than or equal to

```
if(ball.y <= 0 || ball.y >= 480) {
    ball.reverseY();
}
```

greater than or equal to

Oh no! The ball's vanished!

Resetting the Game

What happens if a player misses a shot? We need the game to reset the position and the speed of the ball to what it was at the start of the game. Otherwise, you can't keep playing! We need a function that repositions the ball back in the middle of the board:

reset function

```
reset: function() {
    this.x = 320;
    this.y = 240;
    this.xSpeed = 2;
    this.ySpeed = 0;
},
```

We can then use an if statement to call the reset function if the ball is less than (<) zero pixels or greater than (>) 640 pixels (the width of the board).

```
if(ball.x < 0 || ball.x > 640) {
    ball.reset();
}
```

reset function call

153

GAME BUILD 7 ▶ FINISHING THE BALL

Make the ball speed up when it collides with the paddles or the sides of the board.

1. Open your saved **tennis6.html** file and add some new code to the updateGame function. Every time the ball hits a paddle, we need to call the new code that will speed up the movement of the ball across the screen:

```
if(collidedWithPlayer || collidedWithAi) {
    ball.reverseX();
    ball.modifyXSpeedBy(0.25);
}
```

2. Now to make the ball bounce, we need to modify the ySpeed of the ball, so it will move up and down. To do this, we need to get the speedModifier from the paddle the ball just collided with and store it in a variable:

```
if(collidedWithPlayer || collidedWithAi) {
    ball.reverseX();
    ball.modifyXSpeedBy(0.25);
    var speedUpValue = collidedWithPlayer ? player.speedModifier : ai.speedModifier;
}
```

3. Then increase the speed of the ball with the speedModifier of the paddle. Remember: if the paddle is still, the ball won't bounce any faster.

```
if(collidedWithPlayer || collidedWithAi) {
    ball.reverseX();
    ball.modifyXSpeedBy(0.25);
    var speedUpValue = collidedWithPlayer ? player.speedModifier : ai.speedModifier;
    ball.modifyYSpeedBy(speedUpValue);
}
```

 At this point, the ball will still travel through the game board walls. If you save your code as **tennis7.html** and open it in your browser, you will see that the ball drops off the board.

4. We need to add collision detection to the top and bottom of the board at the start of the `updateGame` function:

```
function updateGame() {
    ball.x += ball.xSpeed;
    ball.y += ball.ySpeed;
    if(ball.y <= 0 || ball.y >= 480) {
        ball.reverseY();
    }
    var collidedWithPlayer = player.hasCollidedWith(ball);
```

 Save your file and refresh your browser. The ball will start bouncing. You can beat the other player because the AI isn't playing against you yet. Once you manage to score a point, though, the ball disappears!

5. Add the reset function to the ball to stop it from dropping off the screen:

```
var ball = {
    x: 320, y: 240, radius: 3, xSpeed: 2, ySpeed: 0,
    reverseX: function() {
        this.xSpeed *= -1;
    },
    reverseY: function() {
        this.ySpeed *= -1;
    },
    reset: function() {
        this.x = 320;
        this.y = 240;
        this.xSpeed = 2;
        this.ySpeed = 0;
    },
    isBouncing: function() {
```

> We need the ball to reset so you can keep playing!

continues

6. Now, in the same way we added collision detection to the top and bottom, we can add code to our function to make sure that when our ball goes beyond the paddles (either with an x position less than zero or greater than 640 pixels), we can reset the ball:

```
function updateGame() {
    ball.x += ball.xSpeed;
    ball.y += ball.ySpeed;
    if(ball.x < 0 || ball.x > 640) {
        ball.reset();
    }
    if(ball.y <= 0 || ball.y >= 480) {
        ball.reverseY();
    }
}
```

7. Save your file and refresh your browser. Your game should now be working, except the AI paddle. Let's code the AI now!

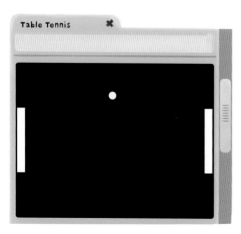

Almost done! We just need to code the AI and our game is finished.

CODING THE AI PADDLE

We need someone to play against! Let's learn how to code a piece of basic AI so the computer becomes the second player and can control the paddle by itself.

What is AI?

Intelligence is how we describe our ability to respond to and learn from new situations. When the player in *Table Tennis* moves the paddle to hit the ball, they are responding to a new situation by making a decision about where to position the paddle. If the player loses a game by making a mistake, our human intelligence enables us to remember what we did wrong and learn from it.

AI, or artificial intelligence, isn't the same as human intelligence. Computers are great at

following detailed instructions but aren't as good at responding to new situations they haven't been programmed to deal with. AI is the process by which humans write programs for computers that try to make them copy human reactions and learning processes as much as possible. Ultimately, it's very difficult to make a computer's intelligence match a human's. Computers and humans don't yet think in the same way.

Calculating AI

The simplest AI we can code is to have the computer always try to position the middle of its paddle at the same x-coordinate as the ball. Because the paddles have a fixed speed and the ball will speed up when it bounces, the player will sometimes be able to win because the computer won't be able to reposition its paddle in time.

We need to add the AI at the end of our `updateGame` function. To work out where the middle of our AI paddle is, we're adding the y-coordinate of the top of the AI paddle to half of the paddle's height (we divide it by two).

Then if the middle of the AI paddle is closer to zero (the top of the screen) than the `ball.y` position, we can move it downward by calling `ai.move` with the keyCode of our down arrow.

If the `aiMiddle` value is nearer to the bottom of our screen than the `ball.y` position, we can move the AI paddle upward by sending the keyCode of the up arrow.

```
                              top of AI paddle     height calculation
var aiMiddle = ai.y + (ai.height / 2);
if(aiMiddle < ball.y) {            division operator
    ai.move(40);       down arrow keyCode
}
if(aiMiddle > ball.y) {
    ai.move(38);
}            up arrow keyCode
```

Code a piece of simple AI to make the second paddle move by itself.

1. Open your **tennis7.html** file. First we need to work out where the middle of the AI paddle is. Add a variable at the end of the updateGame function:

```
    for(var keyCode in heldDown) {
        player.move(keyCode);
    }
    var aiMiddle = ai.y + (ai.height / 2);
}
```

2. Now make the AI paddle move upward or downward depending on the ball's position:

```
    var aiMiddle = ai.y + (ai.height / 2);
    if(aiMiddle < ball.y) {
        ai.move(40);
    }
    if(aiMiddle > ball.y) {
        ai.move(38);
    }
```

Congratulations! We've finished the game!

3. Save your code as **tennis8.html** and open it in your browser. You can now play your game of *Table Tennis* against a very simple AI paddle.

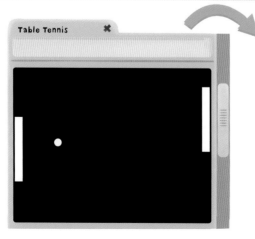

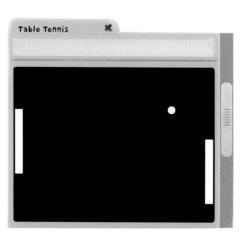

SUPER SKILLS

You can now play *Table Tennis* against simple AI. How can you tidy up your code and change the appearance of the board?

Taking your game further

- 🐱 The numbers 640 and 480 are repeated in the code block. How can you make them tidier? (Hint: You could use variables, or you could make the numbers properties on an object.)

- 🐱 Can you think of a way to change the color of the board, paddles, and ball?

- 🐱 Can you make the ball bigger or smaller? (Hint: Change the radius of the ball.)

- 🐱 Can you think of a better place to work out where the middle of the paddle is? (Hint: The variable `aiMiddle` should probably belong to your `paddle` class.)

- 🐱 How can you code the AI to make mistakes? (Hint: Use `Math.random` from Mission 2 to make the paddle go the wrong way.)

Future game builds

Table Tennis is a real-time sports game that relies on the player's reaction times to win the game. The same kind of simple controls—scrolling up and down or left and right—can be used to make games like *Space Invaders*, *Asteroids*, and many other real-time action games.

```html
<!DOCTYPE html>
<html>
    <head>
        <title>Table Tennis</title>
    </head>
    <body>
        <canvas id="canvas" width="640" height="480"></canvas>
        <script>
            var canvas = document.getElementById("canvas")
            var ctx = canvas.getContext("2d");
            function paddle(x, y, width, height) {
                this.x = x;
                this.y = y;
                this.width = width;
                this.height = height;
                this.speedModifier = 0;
                this.hasCollidedWith = function(ball) {
                    var paddleLeftWall = this.x;
                    var paddleRightWall = this.x + this.width;
                    var paddleTopWall = this.y;
                    var paddleBottomWall = this.y + this.height;
                    if(ball.x > paddleLeftWall
                        && ball.x < paddleRightWall
                        && ball.y > paddleTopWall
                        && ball.y < paddleBottomWall) {
                            return true;
                    }
                    return false;
                };
                this.move = function(keyCode) {
                    var nextY = this.y;
                    if(keyCode == 40) {
                        nextY += 5;
                        this.speedModifier = 1.5;
                    } else if (keyCode == 38) {
                        nextY += -5;
                        this.speedModifier = 1.5;
                    } else {
```

```
                this.speedModifier = 0;
            }
            nextY = nextY < 0 ? 0 : nextY;
            nextY = nextY + this.height > 480 ? 480 - this.height : nextY;
            this.y = nextY;
        };
    }
    var player = new paddle(5, 200, 25, 100);
    var ai = new paddle(610, 200, 25, 100);
    var ball = {
        x: 320, y: 240, radius: 3, xSpeed: 2, ySpeed: 0,
        reverseX: function() {
            this.xSpeed *= -1;
        },
        reverseY: function() {
            this.ySpeed *= -1;
        },
        reset: function() {
            this.x = 320;
            this.y = 240;
            this.xSpeed = 2;
            this.ySpeed = 0;
        },
        isBouncing: function() {
            return ball.ySpeed != 0;
        },
        modifyXSpeedBy: function(modification) {
            modification = this.xSpeed < 0 ? modification * -1 : modification;
            var nextValue = this.xSpeed + modification;
            nextValue = Math.abs(nextValue) > 9 ? 9 : nextValue;
            this.xSpeed = nextValue;
        },
        modifyYSpeedBy: function(modification) {
            modification = this.ySpeed < 0 ? modification * -1 : modification;
            this.ySpeed += modification;
        }
    };
    function tick() {
        updateGame();
        draw();
        window.setTimeout("tick()", 1000/60);
    }
```

continues

```javascript
function updateGame() {
    ball.x += ball.xSpeed;
    ball.y += ball.ySpeed;
    if(ball.x < 0 || ball.x > 640) {
        ball.reset();
    }
    if(ball.y <= 0 || ball.y >= 480) {
        ball.reverseY();
    }
    var collidedWithPlayer = player.hasCollidedWith(ball);
    var collidedWithAi = ai.hasCollidedWith(ball);
    if(collidedWithPlayer || collidedWithAi) {
        ball.reverseX();
        ball.modifyXSpeedBy(0.25);
        var speedUpValue = collidedWithPlayer ? player.speedModifier : ai.speedModifier;
        ball.modifyYSpeedBy(speedUpValue);
    }
    for(var keyCode in heldDown) {
        player.move(keyCode);
    }
    var aiMiddle = ai.y + (ai.height / 2);
    if(aiMiddle < ball.y) {
        ai.move(40);
    }
    if(aiMiddle > ball.y) {
        ai.move(38);
    }
}
function draw() {
    ctx.fillStyle = "black";
    ctx.fillRect(0, 0, 640, 480);
    renderPaddle(player);
    renderPaddle(ai);
    renderBall(ball);
}
function renderPaddle(paddle) {
    ctx.fillStyle = "white";
    ctx.fillRect(paddle.x, paddle.y, paddle.width, paddle.height);
}
```

```
        function renderBall(ball) {
            ctx.beginPath();
            ctx.arc(ball.x, ball.y, ball.radius, 0, 2 * Math.PI, false);
            ctx.fillStyle = "white";
            ctx.fill();
        }
        var heldDown = {};
        window.addEventListener("keydown", function(keyInfo) { heldDown[event.keyCode] =
true; }, false);
        window.addEventListener("keyup", function(keyInfo) { delete heldDown[event.keyCode]; },
false);
        tick();
    </script>
  </body>
</html>
```

ENDLESS RUNNER

- USE PROCEDURAL GENERATION TO CREATE THE GAME WORLD

- MAKE THE GAME SCROLL ACROSS THE SCREEN

- ADD GRAVITY SO THE PLAYER CAN JUMP AND FALL

- MAKE THE GAME HARDER OVER TIME

Mission Brief

To	me@getcoding.com
Cc	Ruby; Rusty; Grace; Scratch
Subject	Mission 4 brief

Hey,

The countdown to the hackathon has begun! We've only got one day to go before we take on SaberTooth Studios, and we need to start coding our fourth game. I hope this is going to be the one that wins it for the Lucky Cat Club! If we get it right, there will be no doubt we deserve that trophy.

In this mission, we are going to code an endless runner game called *Run!* Endless runners are simple but really fun to play. You have to jump from platform to platform and try to avoid obstacles. The controls are very simple, often just a jump button, and you can only move forward. But the games are addictive and exciting to play. My favorite is *Cheetah Chase,* and I'm really proud of my highest score. It took me a long time to get that good! Now I can't wait to code my own version of the game.

I'm going to code the game world, the player, and platforms of all different sizes. The game will look quite basic because the plan for the final mission is that we will all work together to build a similar game, but with more exciting graphics and sound effects. It's a race against time now to be ready to take on SaberTooth Studios. I hope you're ready to code! On your mark, get set, go!

Purr-fect wishes,

Markus

THE DEVELOPER'S
DICTIONARY
Your Guide to Games and
Gaming

Endless Runner

From the Developer's Dictionary: Your Guide to Games and Gaming

This entry is about the genre Endless Runner. For other similar games, see Platforms.

Endless runner (or infinite runner) games rose to popularity at the same time as smartphones and tablets. Although concepts in them can be traced back to platform games in arcades in the 1980s, the first widely acknowledged example of an endless runner game was the 2009 blockbuster release *Canabalt* for smartphones.

Endless Runner

Genre:	Endless runner
Mode:	Single-player
First release:	Canabalt (2009)
Playing time:	2 minutes or more (level-dependent)
Skills required:	Quick reactions and observation

Endless runner games need only one button to play, which is normally a single jump button. The player can only move forward and has no control over their speed. The challenge is for the player to try to stay alive for as long as possible by jumping over <u>obstacles</u> and avoiding falling into traps. The game will get faster as the player progresses through the levels. Each level brings new challenges, and the only way for the game to end is if the player dies.

Endless runner games work well on smartphones and tablets because you can control the player by simply tapping on the screen at the right time. This makes the games easy to play on the go. Trying to reach a higher level and increase your score also makes them addictive experiences.

Other famous endless runner games for smartphones and tablets are _Temple Run_, _Jetpack Joyride_, and _Robot Unicorn Attack_. _Temple Run_ has had more than 100 million downloads and been played more than 10 billion times. Elements of the genre have become popular in other games too.

ENDLESS RUNNER

Endless runner games are a type of platform game. The version we are going to code will have a single control that allows the player to jump up onto the platforms. The challenge in the game is that the player has to stay alive for as many levels as they can. If they crash into a platform by not jumping in time, they die.

Endless runners are different from the other games we've coded so far. They use procedural generation to create the game world. This means that instead of programming the level by hand, as we've done in *Snake* and *Table Tennis*, we need to write code that will automatically program the next level as the player is playing.

The Game Build

The rules for our endless runner game are very simple. The player runs through the game world, jumping onto platforms as they go. The challenge is to time the jumps so the player doesn't crash into the edge of the platform. If the player crashes, the game ends. The game is made harder by the fact that the longer the player survives, the faster they run. This means that the timing of the jumps gets trickier as the game progresses.

In our version of an endless runner game, we're going to make the player jump when any key on the keyboard is pressed. We're going to add

gravity and collision detection to the player. We also have to write code that generates the floor the player runs along. The platforms need to keep changing in size to make the game a challenge for the player. We'll keep track of the player's speed, as well as the distance they've traveled, so they can try to beat their previous score. At the end of the mission, the finished game will look like this:

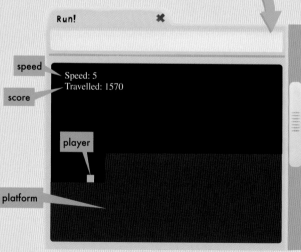

This looks like a great Game Build!

GENERATING THE FIRST TILE

In our endless runner, the player must run and jump over platforms. These platforms form the floor of our game world and are made up of individual **tiles** of different heights. Because we're going to be using procedural generation to create the game world—remember: that's when code is used to create the levels as we play—we need to start by generating the floor of the game world, which means coding the first tile.

CODE WORDS A tile-based game uses small graphic squares, laid out in a grid, to create the game world. Each individual square is called a **TILE**.

Creating the Floor

As in *Table Tennis*, where we created the player and AI objects from functions, we're going to create a floor function to code our floor tiles:

```
function floor(x, height) {
    this.x = x;          tile's left corner
    this.width = 700;    tile width
    this.height = height; tile height
}
```

floor function

Our floor function takes two arguments: x and height. The location of the floor tile's top left corner will be given in the x-coordinate. The width of the game will be 700 pixels. The height will be how tall the floor tile is in pixels. This value will change during the course of the game because we want the tiles to be different heights.

The Game World

We want to create the game world as an object with several properties. Our world object will be simple to start with. It contains the width and height of a <canvas>, which is set to 640 and 480 pixels. It contains a gravity property set to 10 pixels per tick

```
var world = {          world object
    height: 480,       height property
    width: 640,        width property
    gravity: 10,       gravity property
    floorTiles: [      floor tile property    array
        new floor(0, 140)
    ]
};                     new operator
```

that we'll use later. It also contains an array called floorTiles that we're using to create the first tile.

Inside the floorTiles array, we're calling the floor function we've just defined, with 0 and 140 as arguments. We are using the new operator to create the first floor-tile object, starting at the left of our canvas. The tile will have an x location of 0 pixels and be 140 pixels high.

Using a Loop to Draw the Tiles

We want tiles to be continuously generated as our game runs, so we're going to use a for loop to keep creating the tiles in our floorTiles array. The loop will be inside the world object. It will be part of a draw function that will draw each tile on the <canvas> as the game runs:

```
draw: function() {
    ctx.fillStyle = "black";
    ctx.fillRect(0, 0, this.width, this.height);
    for(index in this.floorTiles) {
        var tile = this.floorTiles[index];
        var y = world.height - tile.height;
        ctx.fillStyle = "blue";
        ctx.fillRect(tile.x, y, tile.width, tile.height);
    }
}
```

floor tile array

loop

subtract operator

To draw each tile, we need to calculate its y value, which will be how high the tile is. To work this out, we have to take the tile.height and subtract it from the world.height, which is the bottom of our <canvas>. This number will tell us how high on the <canvas> we need to start drawing the tile. Again, this value will change because we want the tiles to be different heights. The loop needs to be able to access the different values in the floorTiles array in order. To do this, we use index and the in keyword to count upward through the array, starting from zero.

We want the game world to have a black background and the floor tiles to be blue. We use the context on our <canvas>, as in our previous missions. To fill in the first blue tile, we use fillRect in the loop, with the tile's x position and our new y value, then tile.width and tile.height.

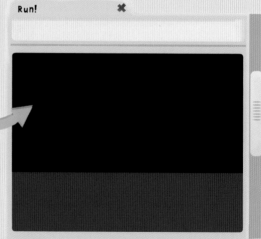

Run!

This is definitely going to beat SaberTooth Studios!

170

GAME BUILD 1 ► GENERATING THE FIRST FLOOR TILE

We need a `<canvas>` to draw on and a loop to generate the tiles.

1. Open your text-editing program. Start by creating a new file called **run1.html**. Add the `<canvas>` element and set its `width` and `height` attributes. Then create a variable called canvas, and assign a reference to the `<canvas>` using `getElementById` and the id attribute. Finally, use `getContext` to put the 2-D rendering context into a variable called ctx.

```html
<!DOCTYPE html>
<html>
<head>
    <title>Run!</title>
</head>
<body>
    <canvas id="canvas" width="640" height="480"></canvas>
    <script>
        var canvas = document.getElementById("canvas");
        var ctx = canvas.getContext("2d");
    </script>
</body>
</html>
```

2. Next we're going to define the floor using a function. Pass the function arguments for the x position and height of the tile:

```js
var ctx = canvas.getContext("2d");
function floor(x, height) {
    this.x = x;
    this.width = 700;
    this.height = height;
}
```

3. We then need to put the floor into the game world. Code an object literal for the world and define the following properties:

```js
    this.height = height;
}
var world = {
    height: 480,
    width: 640,
    gravity: 10,
    floorTiles: [
        new floor(0, 140)
    ]
};
```

4. To make the world and floor appear on the screen, add an empty draw function to the world object:

```js
var world = {
    height: 480,
    width: 640,
    gravity: 10,
    floorTiles: [
        new floor(0, 140)
    ],
    draw: function() {
    }
};
```

continues ➡

5. Fill in the background of the game world in black using the <canvas> fillRect function. Start at (0_0), the top left of our <canvas>. Draw a black rectangle the size of the world by passing this.width and this.height as arguments.

```
draw: function() {
    ctx.fillStyle = "black";
    ctx.fillRect(0, 0, this.width, this.height);
}
```

6. Now we need to expand the draw function to render the tiles in the floorTiles array. We're going to use a for loop to count through each tile in the array. Each tile will be blue, but the width and height will vary.

```
draw: function() {
    ctx.fillStyle = "black";
    ctx.fillRect(0, 0, this.width, this.height);
    for(index in this.floorTiles) {
        var tile = this.floorTiles[index];
        var y = world.height - tile.height;
        ctx.fillStyle = "blue";
        ctx.fillRect(tile.x, y, tile.width, tile.height);
    }
}
```

7. The final thing we need to do is make the game tick. Add a tick function underneath the world object that uses setTimeout to call itself 60 times a second. Then call the draw function to make sure the drawing code runs. Finally, we need to add a call to the new function to start the game.

```
function tick() {
    world.draw();
    window.setTimeout("tick()", 1000/60);
}
tick();
</script>
```

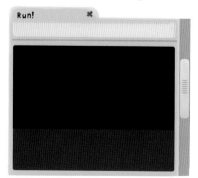

8. Save your file and open it in your browser. You will see the game world on-screen.

MAKING THE GAME SCROLL

The secret to making an endless runner game is that the player doesn't actually move through the world. The illusion of movement is created by making the background graphics move across the screen while the player stays still. As our code generates the floor tiles, we need them to **scroll** from the right side of the screen to the left, which will create the impression that the player is moving forward. We also need code to continuously create new tiles on the right side of the screen as the player "moves."

CODE WORDS
To **SCROLL** means to move text or graphics in a particular direction on a computer screen in order to view different parts of them.

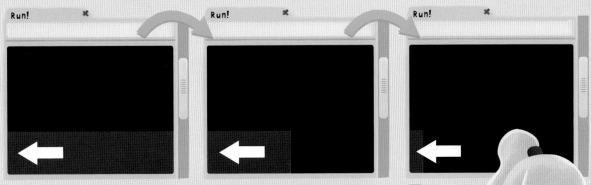

Look at the tile scrolling across the screen!

Using a Loop to Make the Tile Scroll

We need another for loop to make the floor tile scroll across the screen. The loop looks like this:

```
moveFloor: function() {
    for(index in this.floorTiles) {
        var tile = this.floorTiles[index];
        tile.x -= this.speed;
        this.distanceTravelled += this.speed;
    }
},
```

count through array

current tile position

shift tile to left

loop

how far player has traveled

We're looping through the tiles in the array and changing the tile.x position (the position on the x-axis across the screen).

Then we're subtracting (-=) a new speed property from the current tile.x position. This will shift the tile across the screen to the left every time the game ticks.

Finally, we're adding (+=) the current speed to a new distanceTravelled property each time we move our tile. This is so we can keep track of how far the player has traveled across the floor.

Make the floor tile scroll from the right side of the screen to the left.

1. Open up your saved **run1.html** file. To make the tile scroll, we need to add a few new properties to the `world` object: speed and `distanceTravelled`. To begin with, we're going to set speed to 5, and `distanceTravelled` to zero.

```
var world = {
    height: 480,
    width: 640,
    gravity: 10,
    speed: 5,
    distanceTravelled: 0,
    floorTiles: [
```

2. Now we need to add a function that will make the floor scroll. Add a `moveFloor` function into the `world` object:

```
distanceTravelled: 0,
floorTiles: [
    new floor(0, 140)
],
moveFloor: function() {
},
```

3. Just as we did in the draw function, we need to use a loop in the `moveFloor` function. The loop will move the tile from right to left.

```
moveFloor: function() {
    for(index in this.floorTiles) {
        var tile = this.floorTiles[index];
        tile.x -= this.speed;
        this.distanceTravelled += this.speed;
    }
},
```

4. Next add a new `tick` function to the `world` object. Start off by calling the `moveFloor` function, so that each time the game ticks, the floor tile moves.

```
tick: function() {
    this.moveFloor();
},
draw: function() {
```

5. Finally, we're going to add a call to `world.tick` to the top of our main `tick` function. Every time the game ticks, the world ticks, and the game is drawn on-screen.

```
function tick() {
    world.tick();
    world.draw();
    window.setTimeout("tick()", 1000/60);
}
tick();
```

Yay! The game is moving!

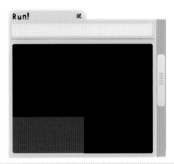

Run!

6. Save your code as **run2.html** and open it in your browser. Watch the floor tile scroll across the screen!

At the moment, we only have a single tile and the floor vanishes off our screen very quickly. We need to make the game more complicated by adding a continuous run of new tiles.

GENERATING MORE TILES

To make the game endless, we need to generate a new tile every time the game scrolls. But we want to do this efficiently so the browser doesn't run out of memory by making thousands of tiles that are never seen by the player. We need to create a function that we can use for our procedural generation code.

Finding the Position for the Next Tile

We want to add our next tile to the right side of our current tile. The new function looks like this:

```
addFutureTiles: function() {
    var previousTile = this.floorTiles[this.floorTiles.length - 1];
    var randomHeight = Math.floor(Math.random() * this.highestFloor) + 20;
    var leftValue = (previousTile.x + previousTile.width);
},
```

access floor tile array

height of new tile

position for new tile

First we have to access the current last tile in our `floorTiles` array. The `length` counts how many tiles already exist in the array, but because `length` starts counting from the number 1, whereas our `floorTiles` array started counting from zero, we need to subtract 1 to make sure we definitely find the last tile. Then we're generating a random height for each new tile by using `Math.random` with the `this.highestFloor` value to set the biggest possible random number. We're then making sure the number is always bigger than 20 pixels, so that the player can see the tiles. Then we calculate the next tile's `leftValue` by adding the last tile's x value to its width value. This tells us where the far right edge of the last tile is: the exact place we need to put our new tile.

Creating the Next Tile

Once we've generated a random height and new position, we need to create the new floor tile.
To do this, we call the floor and pass the leftValue and randomHeight as arguments:

```
addFutureTiles: function() {
    var previousTile = this.floorTiles[this.floorTiles.length - 1];
    var randomHeight = Math.floor(Math.random() * this.highestFloor) + 20;
    var leftValue = (previousTile.x + previousTile.width);
    var next = new floor(leftValue, randomHeight);
    this.floorTiles.push(next);
},
```

new operator

floor function call

push method

We are using the new operator with the floor function to
create a new tile. Then we can use the push method to add
the new tile to the end of the floorTiles array. The next time
the world ticks and draws, a new tile will be drawn on-screen
immediately after the previous one.

Look at the new tile!

Cleaning up the Tiles

The problem with generating a new tile every tick
(which is 60 times a second) is that we create
lots of tiles that are going to scroll off the screen
and never be seen by the player. We don't want
to waste the browser's memory by making it
remember things it doesn't need to draw. Luckily,
we can use a for loop to go through each of our
tiles and check if they have already left the screen.

```
cleanOldTiles: function() {
    for(index in this.floorTiles) {
        if(this.floorTiles[index].x <= -this.floorTiles[index].width) {
            this.floorTiles.splice(index, 1);
        }
    }
},
```

loop

if statement

splice method

position in array

4

The loop uses a complex if statement to work out where the tile is currently positioned. The statement checks if the current floor tile's x value is less than or equal to (<=) its width off the left side of the screen. We're doing this by checking if the value of our tile is less than or equal to (<=) the following:

- this.floorTiles[index].width

This means that if the tile has a width of 700 pixels (as we set in our floor function), when it is 700 pixels off the left of the <canvas> and so has an x value of -700, we'll remove it from the floorTiles array. We do this using the splice method and the index to give the position in the array.

Generating the Right Number of Tiles

We're currently generating 60 tiles a second, which is more than we need. We only need the next tile ahead of the player and the previous tile that the player has jumped onto. Let's slow down the tile generation:

```
if(this.floorTiles.length >= 3) {
    return;
}          guard clause
```

By adding a **guard clause** to the start of our addFutureTiles function, we generate new tiles only if we have fewer than three tiles available (the last tile, our current tile, and our next tile).

CODE WORDS — A **GUARD CLAUSE** is a short if statement that stops the rest of the code from running if it is true.

We now have tiles of different heights that scroll forever without clogging up the browser's memory. This is procedural generation in action!

GAME BUILD 3 ► GENERATING MORE TILES

Keep the game scrolling by adding more tiles of varying heights to the left side of the screen.

1. Open up your saved **run2.html** file. Add a new property called highestFloor to the world object, and set it to 240 pixels. We're not going to let any of our tiles get taller than halfway up our screen.

```
var world = {
    height: 480,
    width: 640,
    gravity: 10,
    highestFloor: 240,
    speed: 5,
```

continues ►

2. In the world object, underneath the moveFloor function, create a new function called addFutureTiles. We're going to put the procedural generation code in here to create new tiles as we play the game.

```
        this.distanceTravelled += this.speed;
    }
},
addFutureTiles: function() {
},
```

3. We need to add our next tile to the right side of our current tile. Generate a random height for the new tile to keep the player guessing:

```
addFutureTiles: function() {
    var previousTile = this.floorTiles[this.floorTiles.length - 1];
    var randomHeight = Math.floor(Math.random() * this.highestFloor) + 20;
    var leftValue = (previousTile.x + previousTile.width);
},
```

4. Now create the next tile using the new operator with the floor function. Pass the leftValue and randomHeight as arguments to the new tile. Use the push method to add the new tile to the array:

```
addFutureTiles: function() {
    var previousTile = this.floorTiles[this.floorTiles.length - 1];
    var randomHeight = Math.floor(Math.random() * this.highestFloor) + 20;
    var leftValue = (previousTile.x + previousTile.width);
    var next = new floor(leftValue, randomHeight);
    this.floorTiles.push(next);
},
```

5. Make sure we call addFutureTiles by adding a call in our world.tick function:

> We don't want to slow the game down!

```
tick: function() {
    this.addFutureTiles();
    this.moveFloor();
},
```

6. Now clean up the tiles that have scrolled off the screen so the array doesn't get too big. Add a new function under addFutureTiles called cleanOldTiles. Use a loop and an if statement to check if the tile has left the screen. Remember to close all the braces.

```
cleanOldTiles: function() {
    for(index in this.floorTiles) {
        if(this.floorTiles[index].x <= -this.floorTiles[index].width) {
            this.floorTiles.splice(index, 1);
        }
    }
},
tick: function() {
```

7. Just as with our addFutureTiles call, we need to make sure we call cleanOldTiles at the start of our tick function:

```
tick: function() {
    this.cleanOldTiles();
    this.addFutureTiles();
    this.moveFloor();
},
```

8. Finally, add a guard clause to the start of the addFutureTiles function to ensure that new tiles are generated only if we have fewer than three tiles available (the last tile, our current tile, and our next tile):

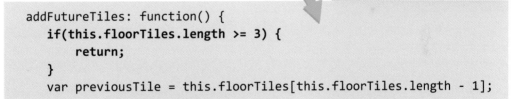

```
addFutureTiles: function() {
    if(this.floorTiles.length >= 3) {
        return;
    }
    var previousTile = this.floorTiles[this.floorTiles.length - 1];
```

9. Save your file as **run3.html** and open it in your browser. The tiles will now scroll from the right to the left of the screen, changing heights as they go.

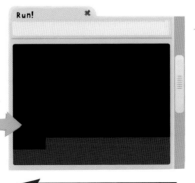
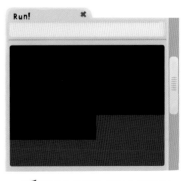

ADDING THE PLAYER

Our game is no fun without a player to control. We'll use an object literal to create the player and give their location in the world. The graphics won't be very complicated: the player will be a simple green square.

The Player Object

Inside the new player object, we need to give the x and y position of the player in the world and set their height and width as properties. The player is going to be a green square that measures 20 pixels by 20 pixels.

```
var player = {          player object
    x: 160,             x position
    y: 340,             y position
    height: 20,         height of player
    width: 20,          width of player
    draw: function() {
        ctx.fillStyle = "green";
        ctx.fillRect(player.x, player.y - player.height, this.height, this.width);
    }
};
```

We have to add a new draw function that calls `fillStyle` to set the player color to green, followed by `fillRect` to draw our player. The player will be rendered in a fixed position on-screen, while the floor scrolls through them.

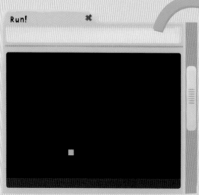

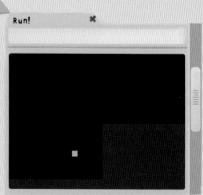

GAME BUILD 4 ► ADDING THE PLAYER

Create the player using an object. Render the player as a green square.

1. Open your saved **run3.html** file. Add a new player object after the world object.
   Set the x, y, height, and width properties of the player as follows:

```
                ctx.fillRect(tile.x, y,  tile.width, tile.height);
        }
    }
};
var player = {
    x: 160,
    y: 340,
    height: 20,
    width: 20,
};
```

Let's code the player!

2. Add a draw function to the player object. Use fillStyle and fillRect to
   make the player into a green square.

```
var player = {
    x: 160,
    y: 340,
    height: 20,
    width: 20,
    draw: function() {
        ctx.fillStyle = "green";
        ctx.fillRect(player.x, player.y - player.height, this.height, this.width);
    }
};
```

continues

3. We also need to call the player.draw function in the main tick function:

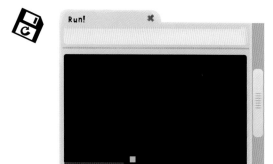

```
function tick() {
    world.tick();
    world.draw();
    player.draw();
    window.setTimeout("tick()", 1000/60);
}
```

4. Save your file as **run4.html** and open it in your browser. We have a player!

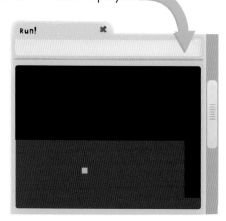

You'll notice that the player doesn't have any collision detection or even obey the laws of gravity. They just float in a fixed position while the floor scrolls underneath or through them. We need to write code to make the player more responsive to the world.

Let's get our player running and jumping!

THE PLAYER'S POSITION

We need to find a way to stop the player from floating in a fixed position. We need to make them respond to the gravity of the floor, either by jumping up or falling down. But first we must find a way to work out the position of the player in the world and how far away they are from the nearest platform.

Finding the Platform Below

We need to find the platform underneath the right corner of the player. Then we need to work out how far below the player that platform is. Let's add a function called getDistanceToFloor to the world object:

```
getDistanceToFloor: function(playerX) {
    for(index in this.floorTiles) {
        var tile = this.floorTiles[index];
        if(tile.x <= playerX && tile.x + tile.width >= playerX) {
            return tile.height;
        }
    }
    return -1;
},
```

`loop` → points to `for(index in this.floorTiles) {`

`if statement` → points to `if(tile.x <= playerX...`

The function is going to take the x location of our player as an argument. We're going to use this to find out which platform is directly underneath the player's x location.

Then we need to work out how high that platform is. To do this, we're going to loop through each of our tiles and use an if statement to check if the player's x value is above or inside the tile. Let's break the if statement down:

🐱 If the tile.x value is less than or equal to (<=) the playerX

🐱 and (&&) if tile.x added to (+) the tile.width (the right side of the tile) is greater than or equal to (>=) the playerX,

🐱 then the tile.height will be returned.

Finding the Height of the Platform

We can find the height of the platform underneath the player by adding a new `applyGravity` function to the `player` object:

```
applyGravity: function() {
    var platformBelow = world.getDistanceToFloor(this.x);
    this.currentDistanceAboveGround = world.height - this.y - platformBelow;
},
```

function call

above ground value

In this function, we're going to call the `getDistanceToFloor` function we've just added with the player's `this.x` value. This will give us the height of the platform. We can store the value in a variable called `platformBelow`.

Now that we have the distance to the floor below the player, we need to work out how far above the floor the player is. This is so we know how far the player needs to fall to land on the platform. To do this, we take the total `world .height` and subtract the player's current `this.y` value and the distance from the floor, which is the value in the `platformBelow` variable. We now know where the player is in the world in relation to the scrolling tiles, and how far they need to fall each time to return to the floor below.

We need to hurry if we're going to finish the game!

How long until the hackathon?

4

GAME BUILD 5 ▶ THE PLAYER'S POSITION

Work out the player's position in relation to the platform below them.

1. Open your saved **run4.html** file. In the `world` object, after the `cleanOldTiles` function, add a function called `getDistanceToFloor`:

```
getDistanceToFloor: function(playerX) {
    return -1;
},
```

2. Now we need to add a loop and an if statement to work out which platform is underneath the player:

```
getDistanceToFloor: function(playerX) {
    for(index in this.floorTiles) {
        var tile = this.floorTiles[index];
        if(tile.x <= playerX && tile.x + tile.width >= playerX) {
        }
    }
    return -1;
},
```

> I have high hopes for our player!

3. Because we're looping through all the tiles, we can return as soon as we find the tile underneath the player:

```
getDistanceToFloor: function(playerX) {
    for(index in this.floorTiles) {
        var tile = this.floorTiles[index];
        if(tile.x <= playerX && tile.x + tile.width >= playerX) {
                return tile.height;
        }
    }
    return -1;
},
```

continues ⟶

4. Inside the `player` object, add an `applyGravity` function that gives the height of the platform underneath the player. Put that value into a variable called `platformBelow`:

```
height: 20,
width: 20,
applyGravity: function() {
    var platformBelow = world.getDistanceToFloor(this.x);
},
```

5. Now that we have the platform below the player, we need to work out how far above the platform the player is. This is so we know how far the player needs to fall.

```
applyGravity: function() {
    var platformBelow = world.getDistanceToFloor(this.x);
    this.currentDistanceAboveGround = world.height - this.y - platformBelow;
},
```

6. Above the draw function in the player object, create a `tick` function that calls `applyGravity`:

```
tick: function() {
    this.applyGravity();
},
draw: function()
```

7. We also need to call our `player.tick` function in the main `tick` function that's called 60 times a second:

```
function tick() {
    player.tick();
    world.tick();
    world.draw();
    player.draw();
    window.setTimeout("tick()", 1000/60);
}
```

8. Save your file as **run5.html**. You won't see any changes to your game yet, but as the player moves, the code keeps track of how far from the floor the player is. We now need to write code to make the player respond to the gravity of the platforms, by either falling off them or jumping on them.

ADDING GRAVITY

Now that we know where the player is in the scrolling game world, we need to add gravity to our game. When the player is on the edge of a platform, they need to fall off it onto the platform below. We also want the player to be able to jump up from one platform to another.

Making the Player Fall

We need to add some new gravity functions to the player. The first function will process the gravity and make the player move:

```
processGravity: function() {
    this.y += world.gravity;
},
```

Every time processGravity is called, we're going to make the player fall by adding the value of the gravity in the world object to the player's y value, which is their vertical location in the world. This will move the player downward.

Stop the Player from Falling through the Floor

Because we're now making the player fall downward, we need to use the getDistanceToFloor function in the world object to make sure our player can't fall through the floor of the platform below them:

```
processGravity: function() {
    this.y += world.gravity;
    var floorHeight = world.getDistanceToFloor(this.x, this.width);
    var topYofPlatform = world.height - floorHeight;
    if(this.y > topYofPlatform) {
        this.y = topYofPlatform;
    }
},
```

if statement

As the player falls, we need to find the top of the new platform (the floor) that the player will stand on. We call getDistanceToFloor with the player's current x location and this.width. From the floorHeight returned to us by our function, we can work out the y value of the platform by subtracting the floorHeight from the world.height.

Then we can see if the player has been pulled down by gravity below the floor. If the player's y value is greater (closer to the bottom of the screen) than the topYofPlatform variable, we simply set our player's y value to the top of the platform's y value. This means they can't fall through the floor.

GAME BUILD 6 ▶ ADDING GRAVITY

Add gravity to your game to make the player fall off the platforms.

1. Open up your saved **run5.html** file. Add a processGravity function to the player object underneath the applyGravity function:

```
processGravity: function() {
},
```

2. Make sure gravity has an effect on the player by adding the value of world .gravity to the player's this.y value:

```
processGravity: function() {
    this.y += world.gravity;
},
```

3. Now stop the player from falling through the floor. Use an if statement and the y value of the top of the platform, like this:

```
processGravity: function() {
    this.y += world.gravity;
    var floorHeight = world.getDistanceToFloor(this.x, this.width);
    var topYofPlatform = world.height - floorHeight;
    if(this.y > topYofPlatform) {
        this.y = topYofPlatform;
    }
},
```

4. All that's left is for us to call processGravity every tick. Add the call to the start of the player.tick function:

```
tick: function() {
    this.processGravity();
    this.applyGravity();
},
```

5. Save your file as **run6.html**. Open it in your browser and refresh a few times until a tile is lower than the player. Watch the player fall off the edge and move along the scrolling floor.

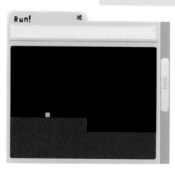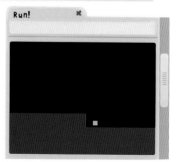

ADDING COLLISION DETECTION

Now that the player can fall off platforms, we should stop them from passing through platforms that are higher than them. We also want the game to stop when the player misses a jump and crashes into the edge of a platform.

Collisions with Platforms

We have to update the applyGravity function to check that the player hasn't fallen lower than the top of a platform. This will happen when a higher platform scrolls past the player.

```
applyGravity: function() {
        var platformBelow = world.getDistanceToFloor(this.x);
        this.currentDistanceAboveGround = world.height - this.y - platformBelow;
        if(this.currentDistanceAboveGround < 0) {
            world.stop();
        }
    },
```

if statement

stop function call

less than operator

The check is as simple as using an if statement to check if this.currentDistanceAboveGround is less than (<) zero. If it is, stop the game by calling a new stop function.

Making the Game Stop

We want the game to stop scrolling and end when the player crashes into a platform. We need to add a stop function to the world object with an autoscroll property.

We can then check in the world.tick function if autoScroll is set to false. If it is, we can return the tick function. This will stop the rest of the world.tick code from running, and the game will end.

```
stop: function() {
    this.autoScroll = false;
},
```

How do we make the game end?

Making the Player Crash

At the moment, when the player meets a platform that's higher than them, the player jumps onto the top of the platform instead of stopping the game. What we actually want to happen is for the game to stop if the player crashes.

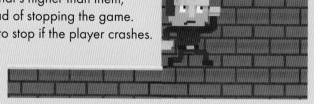

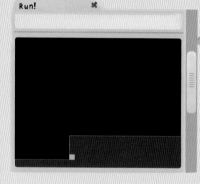

For now, the collision detection code only applies to the top left corner of the player. This means that most of the player can pass through the platform and the processGravity function is applied to the player object, changing the player's y-coordinate and moving the player to the top of the platform. All this happens before the left corner of the player has a chance to even reach the edge of the platform, so the collision detection is not applied. Let's fix this:

```
getDistanceFor: function(x) {
    var platformBelow = world.getDistanceToFloor(x);
    return world.height - this.y - platformBelow;
},
applyGravity: function() {
    this.currentDistanceAboveGround = this.getDistanceFor(this.x);
    var rightHandSideDistance = this.getDistanceFor(this.x + this.width);
    if(this.currentDistanceAboveGround < 0 || rightHandSideDistance < 0) {
        world.stop();
    }
},
```

function call — x value — width — less than operator — or operator

All we've done here is split our original code into two functions. We're putting the existing code in applyGravity into a new function called getDistanceFor and giving it a name.

In the modified applyGravity, we're calculating where the right side of our player is by calling getDistanceFor and passing it two arguments. We're passing the x value plus the width, which equals the right side of our player. We're then using the or operator (||) to check that the this.x value on both the left and right side of the player is not less than (<) zero. The player will now stop when they crash into a wall, and the game will stop scrolling.

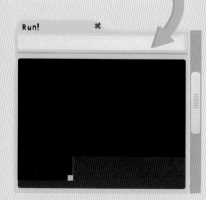

GAME BUILD 7 ► ADDING COLLISION DETECTION

Use collision detection to stop the player from moving through the platforms. Then make the game stop when the player crashes.

1. Open your saved **run6.html** file. Add a check in the applyGravity function to make sure the player hasn't fallen through the platform. If they have, the game will stop.

```
applyGravity: function() {
    var platformBelow = world.getDistanceToFloor(this.x);
    this.currentDistanceAboveGround = world.height - this.y - platformBelow;
    if(this.currentDistanceAboveGround < 0) {
        world.stop();
    }
},
```

2. To make sure the game will stop, add an autoScroll property to the world object. Set it to true by default:

```
var world = {
    height: 480,
    width: 640,
    gravity: 10,
    highestFloor: 240,
    speed: 5,
    distanceTravelled: 0,
    autoScroll: true,
```

3. We also need to create a stop function in the world object. This should set the new autoScroll property to false:

```
floorTiles: [
    new floor(0, 140)
],
stop: function() {
    this.autoScroll = false;
},
```

4. We need to add an if statement to the top of the world.tick function to stop the game when a player crashes:

```
tick: function() {
    if(!this.autoScroll) {
        return;
    }
    this.cleanOldTiles();
    this.addFutureTiles();
    this.moveFloor();
},
```

continues ➡

5. Save your code as **run7.html** and open it in your browser. Watch as the player crashes into a wall. Can you see the bug? Because the collision detection is checking if the left side of the player has passed through a platform (the player.x variable), the front half of the player can pass through it and the player jumps to the top of the platform instead of stopping. Let's fix that.

6. To fix this bug, we're going to create a new function called getDistanceFor in the player object, above the applyGravity function:

```
width: 20,
getDistanceFor: function(x) {
    var platformBelow = world.getDistanceToFloor(x);
    return world.height - this.y - platformBelow;
},
```

This is the code we were previously using in our applyGravity function, just given a namespace.

7. We're now going to change the applyGravity function, because we need to call the code more than once and we don't want to repeat it. Change the code in our applyGravity function as follows:

```
getDistanceFor: function(x) {
    var platformBelow = world.getDistanceToFloor(x);
    return world.height - this.y - platformBelow;
},
applyGravity: function() {
    this.currentDistanceAboveGround = this.getDistanceFor(this.x);
    if(this.currentDistanceAboveGround < 0) {
        world.stop();
    }
},
```

8. Finally, make sure both the right and left sides of the player are being checked:

```
applyGravity: function() {
    this.currentDistanceAboveGround = this.getDistanceFor(this.x);
    var rightHandSideDistance = this.getDistanceFor(this.x + this.width);
    if(this.currentDistanceAboveGround < 0 || rightHandSideDistance < 0) {
        world.stop();
    }
},
```

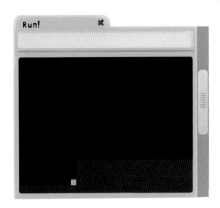

9. Save your file and refresh your browser. The player now collides correctly with the platforms and the game stops.

Now we need to make the player jump!

ADDING JUMPING

We don't have much of a game if the player can't jump. We've made the player fall with gravity, but we need a way to let the user control the player and have them jump onto the platforms. We need to add an eventListener, so when the user presses any key on the board, the player will jump.

Jumping Upward

We need code that allows the player to jump if they're standing on the floor.

```
keyPress: function(keyInfo) {
    var floorHeight = world.getDistanceToFloor(this.x, this.width);
    var onTheFloor = floorHeight == (world.height - this.y);
    if(onTheFloor) {
        this.downwardForce = -8;
    }
},
```

function call

arguments

equal to operator

jump speed per tick

Luckily for us, we already have a function in our world object that will tell us how high the floor is. We need to call world.getDistanceToFloor, passing this.x and this.width as arguments and storing the result in a variable called floorHeight. Then we can determine if the player is standing on the floor by checking if the current floor height is the same as the world height, minus the player's y value.

193

Finally, if a key is pressed and we detect that the player is on the floor, we should set the downwardForce value to −8, which is our jump speed per game tick. We're using a negative number, because while gravity pushes us downward, a negative number here will make the player go upward.

We also need an eventListener to call player.keyPress whenever any keyboard key is pressed. Because all our player can do is jump, we don't need to worry about which keys are pressed:

```
window.addEventListener("keypress", function(keyInfo) { player.keyPress(keyInfo); }, false);
```
eventListener   event   key to store   function call

Falling downward

Once the player can jump up, we also need to make sure they can fall back down again. We need to add some new code to the end of our processGravity function:

```
if(this.downwardForce < 0) {
    this.jumpHeight += (this.downwardForce * -1);
    if(this.jumpHeight >= player.height * 6) {
        this.downwardForce = world.gravity;
        this.jumpHeight = 0;
    }
}
```
multiplication operator

First we need to check if the player is jumping. To do that, we can simply check if the downwardForce value is less than (<) zero. If it is, we're adding the this.downwardForce multiplied by −1 to the jumpHeight, so we can keep track of how high the player has jumped so far.

We're multiplying the downwardForce by −1 to invert the number, turning our negative number, −8, into a positive number, 8.

We then need to set a maximum allowed jump height. We're going to do this by checking if our jumpHeight is greater or equal to (>=) the player.height value multiplied by 6. This means the player can jump six times their height.

Once the player reaches the maximum jump height, we can reset the downwardForce property to world.gravity and reset the jumpHeight property to zero. The player will now jump onto platforms and fall back down again.

Did you notice?

When we multiply a negative number by a negative number, it becomes a positive number.

4

GAME BUILD 8 ► ADDING JUMPING

Make the player jump onto the platforms and then fall back down again.

1. Open your **run7.html** file. First we're going to add downwardForce and jumpHeight properties to our player object. Set downwardForce to world.gravity, and jumpHeight to zero:

```
var player = {
    x: 160,
    y: 340,
    height: 20,
    width: 20,
    downwardForce: world.gravity,
    jumpHeight: 0,
```

2. Add a keyPress function to the player object underneath the processGravity function. We'll leave it empty for the moment, but we're going to add an eventListener to our code to pass any keyboard input into this function.

```
keyPress: function(keyInfo) {
},
```

3. Add the eventListener after the player object and right before the main tick function. Call keyPress whenever any keyboard key is pressed:

```
window.addEventListener("keypress", function(keyInfo) { player.keyPress(keyInfo); }, false);
function tick() {
```

4. We need to add code to the empty keyPress function so that the player can jump upward if they're standing on the floor:

```
keyPress: function(keyInfo) {
    var floorHeight = world.getDistanceToFloor(this.x, this.width);
    var onTheFloor = floorHeight == (world.height - this.y);
    if(onTheFloor) {
        this.downwardForce = -8;
    }
},
```

5. To make sure the processGravity function understands that the player can now move upward as well as downward, we need to modify the function to use our new downwardForce property. Change the first line so it uses this .downwardForce for the number of pixels to add to the this.y value:

```
processGravity: function() {
    this.y += this.downwardForce;
```

195

continues ➡

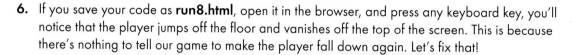
6. If you save your code as **run8.html**, open it in the browser, and press any keyboard key, you'll notice that the player jumps off the floor and vanishes off the top of the screen. This is because there's nothing to tell our game to make the player fall down again. Let's fix that!

7. Add a new if statement to the end of the processGravity function to keep track of how high the player has jumped:

```
this.y = topYofPlatform;
}
if(this.downwardForce < 0) {
    this.jumpHeight += (this.downwardForce * -1);
}
```

8. Then add a second if statement that sets the player's maximum allowed jump height to six times their height:

```
if(this.downwardForce < 0) {
    this.jumpHeight += (this.downwardForce * -1);
    if(this.jumpHeight >= player.height * 6) {
    }
}
```

9. Once the player reaches their maximum jump height, all we need to do is reset the downwardForce property to world.gravity, and reset our jumpHeight property to zero. The code we've already written will make our player fall back to the ground.

```
if(this.downwardForce < 0) {
    this.jumpHeight += (this.downwardForce * -1);
    if(this.jumpHeight >= player.height * 6) {
        this.downwardForce = world.gravity;
        this.jumpHeight = 0;
    }
}
```

10. Save your file and refresh your browser. Your player will now be able to jump onto platforms of a certain height and then fall back down again.

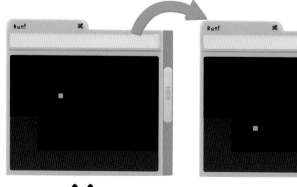

MAKING ALL THE JUMPS POSSIBLE

We need to make sure the player can actually jump onto all the platforms we're generating.
At the moment, the player can only jump onto ones that are a certain height.

Changing the Platform Height

We need to revisit the addFutureTiles function. We've set our
player's maximum jump to six times the player's height, so we
need to make sure that none of the platforms we generate are
higher than this. Our revised function will look like this:

> Let's make
> sure the game
> is possible to
> play!

```
addFutureTiles: function() {
    if(this.floorTiles.length >= 3) {
        return;
    }
    var previousTile = this.floorTiles[this.floorTiles.length - 1];
    var biggestJumpableHeight = previousTile.height + player.height * 3.5;
    if(biggestJumpableHeight > this.highestFloor) {
        biggestJumpableHeight = this.highestFloor;
    }
    var randomHeight = Math.floor(Math.random() * biggestJumpableHeight) + player.height;
    var leftValue = (previousTile.x + previousTile.width);
    var next = new floor(leftValue, randomHeight);
    this.floorTiles.push(next);
},
```

`new variable`

`random generation`

`maximum height value`

We're making sure that the player can jump the randomHeight number we generate. We
need to add a variable that stores the biggest possible jump height. Then we're taking the
last platform's height and adding the player's height multiplied by (*) 3.5. We're using
3.5 because the player can jump six times higher than their
height, so this makes sure the player will always be able to
make our jumps. We can then use an if statement to check
the new value and update the random generation to use it
too.

GAME BUILD 9 ► MAKING THE JUMPS POSSIBLE

Change the height of the platforms so they are always possible for the player.

1. Open up your saved **run8.html** file. In the addFutureTiles in the world object, we need to change the calculation for the biggest jumpable height as follows:

```
addFutureTiles: function() {
    if(this.floorTiles.length >= 3) {
        return;
    }
    var previousTile = this.floorTiles[this.floorTiles.length - 1];
    var biggestJumpableHeight = previousTile.height + player.height * 3.5;
    if(biggestJumpableHeight > this.highestFloor) {
        biggestJumpableHeight = this.highestFloor;
    }
    var randomHeight = Math.floor(Math.random() * this.highestFloor) + 20;
```

2. Change our random generation to use the new value in the biggestJumpableHeight variable and the player.height:

```
var randomHeight = Math.floor(Math.random() * biggestJumpableHeight) + player.height;
```

3. Save your code as **run9.html** and open it in your browser. Now we know for certain that no jump heights will be generated that the player can't reach. Our game is fair for the player.

Watch your player jump!

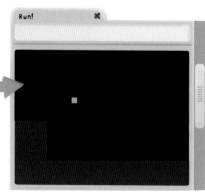

Run!

INCREASING THE DIFFICULTY OVER TIME

In an endless runner game, difficulty is increased over time by increasing the speed at which the game scrolls. To do this, we need to track how many platforms the player has jumped past, and make sure we give our game a maximum speed so it doesn't get so fast that the player cannot play. We want to show the speed and distance on-screen, so the player can keep track of their score.

Increasing the Speed

We're going to speed up the game by one extra pixel per tick every time we pass three tiles. We need a new if statement:

remainder operator

increment operator

and operator

```
if(this.tilesPassed % 3 == 0 && this.speed < this.maxSpeed) {
    this.speed++;
}
```

We're working out if the number of tiles we have passed can divide equally by three, using the % (remainder) operator. If there is a remainder of zero when we divide this number by three, we know we've just passed a third tile. We're also going to check that our this.speed property is less than (<) this.maxSpeed so we don't make the game too fast.

When we've passed a third tile and haven't yet reached our maxSpeed, we're just going to add to this.speed using the increment (++) operator. The game will speed up by one pixel per tick every three tiles.

Showing the Speed and Distance

The only thing left to do is show the player how well they are doing by displaying their current speed and distance traveled on the screen. Remember: the player is trying to go as far as they can.

We're going to use a new <canvas> API called fillText to do this. This will write words on your <canvas> at the x and y locations you give it.

First we set our text color to white using fillStyle. Then we set the font and size for our text by calling:

This is just like setting a font in a CSS style sheet!

size   font

```
ctx.font = "28px Arial";
```

Then we're going to write our text on the screen by using the fillText function, which takes the following arguments:

> We've nearly finished the game!

text
position on screen

```
ctx.fillText("Our text here", x, y);
```

We'll add these new APIs to the draw function as follows:

speed value
distance traveled value

```
ctx.fillStyle = "white";
ctx.font = "28px Arial";
ctx.fillText("Speed: " + this.speed, 10, 40);
ctx.fillText("Travelled: " + this.distanceTravelled, 10, 75);
```

You'll notice that the text we're using is just our labels, with our speed and distanceTravelled values rendered as text. We've picked an x and y value near the top of the screen to position the text. Both lines of text will be 10 pixels from the left of the screen, so will have the same x values. They have different y values so that they won't get drawn on top of each other.

Our game is now finished! The longer the player is alive, the faster the game will scroll. And the player will be able to keep track of their progress by seeing their speed and distance traveled.

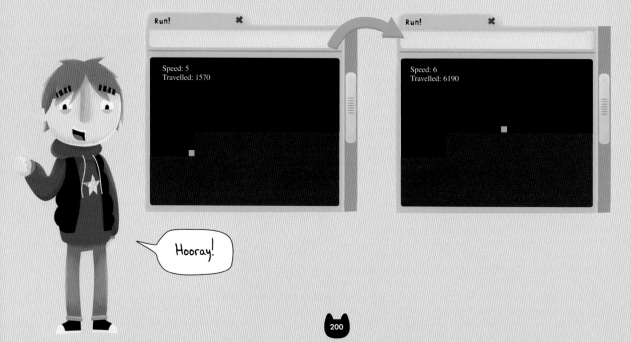

Hooray!

200

GAME BUILD 10 ► INCREASING THE SPEED

Make the game speed up over time and show the player's speed and distance traveled on-screen.

1. Open your saved **run9.html** file. Add maxSpeed and tilesPassed properties to the world object. Set our maxSpeed to 15 and tilesPassed to start with zero.

```
var world = {
    height: 480,
    width: 640,
    gravity: 10,
    highestFloor: 240,
    speed: 5,
    distanceTravelled: 0,
    maxSpeed: 15,
    tilesPassed: 0,
    autoScroll: true,
```

2. We now need to modify our cleanOldTiles function to keep track of the number of tiles the player has jumped over. Add to the value of this.tilesPassed using the increment operator (++) each time we clean a tile away:

```
cleanOldTiles: function() {
    for(index in this.floorTiles) {
        if(this.floorTiles[index].x <= -this.floorTiles[index].width) {
            this.floorTiles.splice(index, 1);
            this.tilesPassed++;
        }
    }
},
```

continues →

3. Next we need to add the code to speed our game up by one extra pixel per tick, every three tiles:

```
cleanOldTiles: function(){
    for(index in this.floorTiles) {
        if(this.floorTiles[index].x <= -this.floorTiles[index].width) {
            this.floorTiles.splice(index, 1);
            this.tilesPassed++;
            if(this.tilesPassed % 3 == 0 && this.speed < this.maxSpeed) {
                this.speed++;
            }
        }
    }
},
```

4. We're going to use the new <canvas> APIs at the end of our world.draw function to display the player's speed and how far they have traveled through the game.

```
            ctx.fillRect(tile.x, y, tile.width, tile.height);
        }
        ctx.fillStyle = "white";
        ctx.font = "28px Arial";
        ctx.fillText("Speed: " + this.speed, 10, 40);
        ctx.fillText("Travelled: " + this.distanceTravelled, 10, 75);
    }
};
```

5. Save your code as **run10.html** and open it in your browser. Let's look at our game now!

We've done it!
We have gravity,
jumping, scrolling,
procedurally
generated levels,
and score keeping.

Well done!

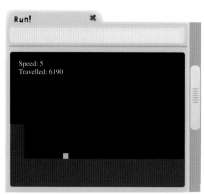

Run!

Speed: 5
Travelled: 6190

SUPER SKILLS

You can run and jump through your game and try to beat your top score.
Now can you make the game harder to play?

Taking your game further

- 🐱 The difficulty of our game comes from how fast the world moves and how good the player is at jumping. Can you work out how to change the difficulty by changing the speed?

- 🐱 Can you work out how to change the player's height?

- 🐱 Can you work out how to change the color of the game world?

- 🐱 There are lots of jumps for the player to make in order to win, but there aren't any pits for the player to fall into. Can you adjust the positions of the platforms to create gaps for the player to avoid?
  (Hint: Change the `leftValue` variable when we generate new floor tiles and adjust the collision detection so the game ends if the player falls into a pit.)

Future game builds

Our endless runner is a real-time platform game that relies on player timing to win. Games like the Mario series, *Donkey Kong*, *Temple Run,* and *Sonic the Hedgehog* all use similar techniques to our endless runner, they just have more sophisticated graphics and sound effects.

```html
<!DOCTYPE html>
<html>
    <head>
        <title>Run!</title>
    </head>
    <body>
        <canvas id="canvas" width="640" height="480"></canvas>
        <script>
            var canvas = document.getElementById("canvas");
            var ctx = canvas.getContext("2d");
            function floor(x, height) {
                this.x = x;
                this.width = 700;
                this.height = height;
            }
            var world = {
                height: 480,
                width: 640,
                gravity: 10,
                highestFloor: 240,
                speed: 5,
                distanceTravelled: 0,
                maxSpeed: 15,
                tilesPassed: 0,
                autoScroll: true,
                floorTiles: [
                    new floor(0, 140)
                 ],
                stop: function() {
                    this.autoScroll = false;
                 },
                moveFloor: function() {
                    for(index in this.floorTiles) {
                        var tile = this.floorTiles[index];
                        tile.x -= this.speed;
                        this.distanceTravelled += this.speed;
                     }
                 },
```

```
addFutureTiles: function() {
  if(this.floorTiles.length >= 3) {
    return;
  }
    var previousTile = this.floorTiles[this.floorTiles.length - 1];
    var biggestJumpableHeight = previousTile.height + player.height * 3.5;
    if(biggestJumpableHeight > this.highestFloor) {
        biggestJumpableHeight = this.highestFloor;
    }
    var randomHeight = Math.floor(Math.random() * biggestJumpableHeight) + player.height;
    var leftValue = (previousTile.x + previousTile.width);
    var next = new floor(leftValue, randomHeight);
    this.floorTiles.push(next);
},
cleanOldTiles: function() {
  for(index in this.floorTiles) {
    if(this.floorTiles[index].x <= -this.floorTiles[index].width) {
      this.floorTiles.splice(index, 1);
      this.tilesPassed++;
      if(this.tilesPassed % 3 == 0 && this.speed < this.maxSpeed) {
        this.speed++;
      }
    }
  }
},
getDistanceToFloor: function(playerX) {
  for(index in this.floorTiles) {
    var tile = this.floorTiles[index];
    if(tile.x <= playerX && tile.x + tile.width >= playerX) {
      return tile.height;
    }
  }
    return -1;
},
tick: function() {
  if(!this.autoScroll) {
    return;
  }
    this.cleanOldTiles();
    this.addFutureTiles();
    this.moveFloor();
},
draw: function() {
  ctx.fillStyle = "black";
```

continues →

```
            ctx.fillRect(0, 0, this.width, this.height);
            for(index in this.floorTiles) {
                var tile = this.floorTiles[index];
                var y = world.height - tile.height;
                ctx.fillStyle = "blue";
                ctx.fillRect(tile.x, y,  tile.width, tile.height);
            }
            ctx.fillStyle = "white";
            ctx.font = "28px Arial";
            ctx.fillText("Speed: " + this.speed, 10, 40);
            ctx.fillText("Travelled: " + this.distanceTravelled, 10, 75);
        }
    };
    var player = {
        x: 160,
        y: 340,
        height: 20,
        width: 20,
        downwardForce: world.gravity,
        jumpHeight: 0,
        getDistanceFor: function(x) {
            var platformBelow = world.getDistanceToFloor(x);
            return world.height - this.y - platformBelow;
        },
        applyGravity: function() {
            this.currentDistanceAboveGround = this.getDistanceFor(this.x);
            var rightHandSideDistance = this.getDistanceFor(this.x + this.width);
            if(this.currentDistanceAboveGround < 0 || rightHandSideDistance < 0) {
                world.stop();
            }
        },
        processGravity: function() {
            this.y += this.downwardForce;
            var floorHeight = world.getDistanceToFloor(this.x, this.width);
            var topYofPlatform = world.height - floorHeight;
            if(this.y > topYofPlatform) {
                this.y = topYofPlatform;
            }
            if(this.downwardForce < 0){
                this.jumpHeight += (this.downwardForce * -1);
                if(this.jumpHeight >= player.height * 6) {
                    this.downwardForce = world.gravity;
                    this.jumpHeight = 0;
                }
            }
```

```
            }
        },
        keyPress: function(keyInfo) {
            var floorHeight = world.getDistanceToFloor(this.x, this.width);
            var onTheFloor = floorHeight == (world.height - this.y);
            if(onTheFloor) {
                this.downwardForce = -8;
            }
        },
        tick: function() {
            this.processGravity();
            this.applyGravity();
        },
        draw: function() {
            ctx.fillStyle = "green";
            ctx.fillRect(player.x, player.y - player.height, this.height, this.width);
        }
    };
    window.addEventListener("keypress", function(keyInfo) { player.keyPress(keyInfo); }, false);
    function tick() {
        player.tick();
        world.tick();
        world.draw();
        player.draw();
        window.setTimeout("tick()", 1000/60);
    }
    tick();
</script>
</body>
</html>
```

> Now we're ready to take on SaberTooth Studios!

mission 5

SIDE-SCROLLING PLATFORMER

- USE THE *GET CODING!* WEBSITE TO CREATE A SIDE-SCROLLING PLATFORM GAME

- DESIGN A LEVEL

- ADD BACKGROUND GRAPHICS

- CREATE ANIMATED PLAYER AND ENEMY CHARACTERS

- ADD SOUND EFFECTS TO THE GAME

Mission Brief

To   me@getcoding.com

Cc   Rusty; Markus; Grace; Scratch

Subject   Mission 5 brief

Hello,

Guess what! We won the Game On Hackathon! We stayed up all night making the finishing touches to the Game Builds. It was scary taking on SaberTooth Studios, but we did it! Our games won all the categories. We couldn't have done it without you!

To celebrate our victory, we want to release our very own game. We thought you might enjoy helping us with one final challenge. So far, all the graphics in our games have been simple colored tiles. Why don't we try coding a game that has super-cool graphics and music? And even better, our game is going to be inspired by our favorite character of all time: Super Mario!

The original Mario games were side-scrolling platform games, where Mario could run and jump through different levels, fighting enemies and avoiding obstacles and traps. We are going to take what Markus learned from coding his endless runner game and then code something very similar, but this time with background graphics, a player that looks like a character, a level that gets harder toward the end, enemies, and sound. Can you guess who our player is going to be? Scratch! And the game will be called *Super Scratch*. Scratch will have to try to dodge the attack of ferocious tigers and avoid falling into pits.

Let's put all our new skills into action and work together on this one. We better jump to it!

Purr-fect wishes,

Ruby, Rusty, Grace, Markus, and Scratch

**THE DEVELOPER'S
DICTIONARY**
Your Guide to Games and
Gaming

Side-Scrolling Platformer

From the Developer's Dictionary: Your Guide to Games and Gaming

This entry is about Platformers. For other Platformers, see Platform Variants.

From the 1980s until the mid-1990s (when 3-D games became popular), **side-scrolling platform games** were the most popular type of games in the world. They inspired the endless runner genre of games, which are similar except they have fewer controls. In endless runners, the player has to run, jump, and fall through levels of increasing complexity, trying to stay alive.

5

Side-Scrolling Platformer

Genre:	Platformer
Mode:	Single-player
First release:	Donkey Kong (1981)
Playing time:	1 minute or more (level-dependent)
Skills required:	Quick reactions and observation

Side-scrolling games are made up of many <u>levels</u>, or <u>maps</u>, that the player has to run and jump through. The player can move forward and backward and has control over their speed. Each level is a different game world with its own layout and normally becomes more complicated the longer the player stays alive. There is also often an <u>enemy</u>, controlled by <u>AI</u>, who tries to stop the player by jumping at them and knocking them off the platform.

The platform game rocketed to popularity in the early 1980s. *Donkey Kong*, by <u>Nintendo</u>, is widely regarded as the first platform game, and it introduced <u>Mario</u>, one of the most famous characters in the history of gaming. He was soon given his own side-scrolling platform game, *Super Mario*. The game was such a success that Mario has become the most enduring and famous video-game character of all time. More than half a billion copies of *Super Mario* have been sold over a thirty-year period. Another famous platformer from this time was <u>Sega</u>'s <u>*Sonic the Hedgehog*</u>.

Originally, the graphics in platformers were 2-D. In 1996, the <u>Nintendo 64</u> console was released and <u>*Super Mario 64*</u> was one of the earliest platformers to have 3-D graphics. The genre has remained popular, being reinvented by each new gaming generation.

SIDE-SCROLLING PLATFORMER

In this mission, we are going to code a side-scrolling platform game. The player is going to be a cat called Scratch. He will have to run and jump through the game world while avoiding falling into pits and being attacked by enemy tigers.

The finished code block will be over 300 lines long. So rather than building the game step-by-step as we did in the previous missions, we are going to run through the key concepts and then you can download the code from the *Get Coding!* website.

The Game Build

This game will have a more complicated game world than the previous missions. In platformers, levels can vary in size, complexity, and theme. Our game is going to have one level, and the player will be an animated cat character called Scratch. We are going to use background graphics to make the game world seem real, as well as music to create atmosphere. There will even be a meow sound effect when Scratch jumps!

We're also going to introduce enemies, in the form of animated tigers, to the game to make it more of a challenge. The tigers will be controlled by the computer using simple AI. More enemies will appear the further through the level Scratch gets.

To win the game, Scratch has to complete the level by jumping across the platforms. He can move forward and backward, as well as jump up and down. If Scratch misses a jump and falls into a pit, he will die and the game will end. Scratch must also avoid being attacked by the tigers. If a tiger touches Scratch, the game will end. To complete the level, Scratch has to jump through the doorway at the end of the obstacles.

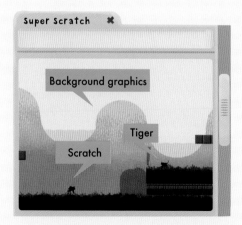

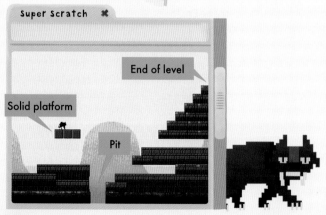

The Game Structure

The basic structure of the game world will be similar to the endless runner in Mission 4. We'll use the `<canvas>` at the start, as in all our other games, so we can draw the world on-screen. And we'll build three JavaScript objects for the main parts of our game. Our basic outline will look like this:

```
                    game object
var game = {
    timer: null,
    finished: false,          code goes in here
    controls: { ... },
    sounds: { ... },       sound and music
    loop: function() { ... },
    start: function() { ... },
    stop: function(reason) { ... }
};            world object
var world = {
    height: 480,
    width: 640,
    gravity: 10,
    distanceTravelled: 0,
    level: null,          collision detection
    collisionMap: null,
    tickCount: 0,
    enemies: [],       level graphics
    loadLevel: function(){ ... },
    getPixelType: function(x, y) { ... },
    tick: function() { ... },
    activateEnemies: function() { ... },
    draw: function() { ... }
};            player object
var player = {            character class
    character: new character( ... ),
    tick: function() { ... },
    processControls: function() { ... },
    draw: function() { ... }
    function character() {...},
    function animation() {...},
    function enemy() {...}
};
```

You will find all the code for this mission on the Get Coding! website.

LEVEL DESIGN

We want to make our graphics more complicated than in the previous missions. The easiest way to design a level is to create it in a graphics program such as Paint, Photoshop, or Paintbrush and then use the image file in the game build.

If you don't want to draw the level, there are plenty of places on the Internet where you can get free pictures to use in your own games. For this mission, you can download all the files from the *Get Coding!* website.

The Game World

When you download the **level.png** file from the *Get Coding!* website, you will see that the level looks like this:

The image file is massive: it's 8,000 pixels wide! This is because our entire level is contained in one image. If we zoom out, the complete level looks like this:

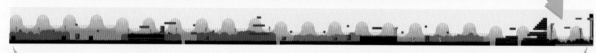

start of the level

Can you see how the obstacles get harder toward the end of the level? It's going to be a real challenge for Scratch to reach that final door. We need to make sure that the gravity and the collision detection in the game world allow Scratch to run and jump over all the obstacles.

end of the level

We load the level in our game world by saving the image file in our JavaScript, then drawing it on the <canvas>. The code we need looks like this:

```
loadLevel: function() {
    this.level = new Image();
    this.level.src = "level.png";
},
draw: function() {
    var drawAtX = this.distanceTravelled * -1;
    drawAtX = drawAtX > 0 ? 0 : drawAtX;
    ctx.drawImage(this.level, drawAtX, 0);
}
```

image file name

draw level on <canvas>

Collision Detection

Level design is also called mapping, because it involves working out how the characters travel through the game world. Our level has multiple floating platforms that Scratch can run across, pits he can fall into, and a final door that he can jump through. To ensure that our code can handle all these eventualities, we have to create a collision map.

Using a collision map allows us to write code for each of the different surfaces in the world. Let's take a look at how the collision map works. As we've already seen, the **level.png** file looks like this:

The collision map shows all the obstacles in the game world.

If you open the collision map file, **map.png**, on the website, you will see that all the surfaces in the level are represented as solid black shapes:

If you zoom all the way out, you'll see exactly where Scratch can and can't run in the game world. Can you guess what the different colors on the collision map mean?

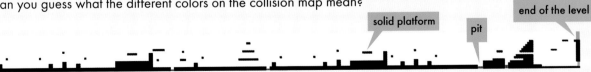

solid platform

pit

end of the level

The black areas represent the floor and platforms Scratch can run and jump across.
The red areas are the pits he must avoid, and the green areas are the doorways to the next level.

THE COLLISION MAP

Because the level and map files are the same dimensions (8,000 pixels wide by 480 pixels high), we can use the colors in the map to work out if Scratch can move through the game world or if he has hit a platform or pit. For example, if he tries to move across a red pixel, we would end the game. To do this, we're going to have to use JavaScript to process the color of the pixels in the map file.

Embedding Images

For our browser to load the pixel colors from our map file, we're going to have to embed the map image data into our JavaScript. We need to convert the bytes in the image file into text that the browser can understand. This is called Base64 encoding.

When we Base64-encode an image, the text is very long—far too long to type in by hand! You can download the Base64-encoded version of our level map, **level-map.txt**, from the *Get Coding!* website.

We'll load the collision map into our game by creating a second "hidden" <canvas> in our loadLevel function. This <canvas> won't be drawn on-screen. Let's take a look at how we expand our function:

```
loadLevel: function() {
    this.level = new Image();
    this.level.src = "level.png";
    var collisionMapImage = new Image();
    collisionMapImage.onload = function (loadEvent) {
        var hiddenCanvas = document.createElement("CANVAS");
        hiddenCanvas.setAttribute("width", this.width);
        hiddenCanvas.setAttribute("height", this.height);
        world.collisionMap = hiddenCanvas.getContext("2d");
        world.collisionMap.drawImage(this, 0, 0);
    };
    collisionMapImage.src = "data:image/png;base64,iVBORw0KGgoA...";
},
```

collision map

hidden <canvas>

Base64-encoded text

Using the Map

We need a function that can use the embedded code to work out what color each of the pixels on the map is. A pixel is the smallest single point of data we can access. Pixels are made up of four pieces of information, often called RGBA, which stands for Red Green Blue Alpha. These are numbers that describe how much color is in each pixel. Let's think about the colors in our collision map as RGBA values:

Color	R	G	B	A	Map
White	255	255	255	255	Space
Black	0	0	0	255	Platform
Red	255	0	0	255	Pit
Green	76	255	0	255	Exit

We can check the colors in our collision map by making sure our RGBA values are correct. Look at this part of the finished code block. The `getImageData` function returns the RGBA values from the map. We can then check the values to decide what to do in the game and code the related functions.

```
getPixelType: function(x, y) {
    var rawData = this.collisionMap.getImageData(x, y, 1, 1).data;
    var mask = rawData[0] + " " + rawData[1] + " " + rawData[2] + " " + rawData[3];
    if (mask == "255 0 0 255") return "pit";
    if (mask == "76 255 0 255") return "exit";
    if (mask == "255 255 255 255") return ".";
    if (mask == "0 0 0 255") return "#";
},
```

getImageData function

red RGBA value for pit

green RGBA value for exit

white RGBA value for space

black RGBA value for platforms

CREATING ANIMATED CHARACTERS

There are two types of animated characters in our game: the Scratch character and the enemy tigers. To make it easy to create these different characters, we're going to create several functions in our code that work as templates, or classes. We will code a class for our animations and characters and then use the information in these classes to create multiple instances of the JavaScript character objects.

Adding Animations

In this mission, we want to use animated graphics to make our player and enemies more interesting. Animations are made by drawing a series of images quickly on the screen, to make it look like the character or object is moving. We can't use the `<canvas>` to draw our animations because it doesn't support animated gifs, but we can build our own class to animate the pictures ourselves.

First we need some pictures to animate—you can download a series of images from the *Get Coding!* website for our main character, Scratch. We can make it look like Scratch is moving by drawing him in different ways:

Each of these images is a single frame of animation. To make our character feel realistic, we are going to use five frames, along with the same five frames flipped in reverse. This will make it look like Scratch is moving forward and backward. We can then create an `animation` class to move the character across the screen. The class works out which frame to draw based on how many ticks have passed in our game, and loads each of the images we need.

The Character Class

Our character class describes the behavior of any character in our game—it could be a player or the enemies—and processes all the interesting things that the characters can do, like move, jump, and fall.

To make the platformer into a challenge, we want to include enemies. We can use all of the logic in the `character` class for the `player` character and the enemy characters, making them really simple to code. The enemies are just another type of character that the computer controls using basic AI.

Because we have a `character` class, our `player` object and our enemy function contain only the information unique to being a player or an enemy, such as AI. Because we've captured all of our more general character behavior in the `character` class, we don't need to repeat our code:

```
var player = {
    character: new character(160, 390, 25, 25,          ← character instance
        new animation("graphics/cat", 5),              ← cat image
        new animation("graphics/cat.backwards", 5)),
    tick: function() { ... },
    processControls: function() { ... },
    draw: function() { this.character.draw(); }
};
function enemy(x, y) {                                  ← character instance
    this.character = new character(x, y, 25, 25,
        new animation("graphics/tiger", 5),            ← enemy image
        new animation("graphics/tiger.backwards", 5))  ← AI
    this.tick = function() { /* Process enemy logic */ },
    this.draw = function() { this.character.draw(); }
}
```

Both the `player` and enemy code has an instance of a `character`—and so reuses all the code inside the `character` class.

ADDING MUSIC AND SOUND EFFECTS

Now we're going to add atmosphere to the game world with sound effects and music. We want background music, as well as a cat's meow every time Scratch jumps.

Adding Sound

I'm the cat's meow!

As with our graphics, we need to download some extra files from the *Get Coding!* website. Playing a sound in HTML5 is as simple as calling:

```
new Audio("sounds/yourfile.mp3").play();
```

We can code a sound object that will play the **meow.wav** file and the **background.mp3** file:

```
var game = {
    sounds: {
        enabled: true,
        jump: function() { this.play("meow.wav"); },              // sound effect
        backgroundMusic: function() { this.play("background.mp3"); },  // background music
        play: function(filename) { if(this.enabled) { new Audio("sounds/" +
filename).play(); } }   // play function
    }
}
```

Our play function does all the work. It checks if sounds are enabled, and if they are, it creates a new audio for the file names we're providing and asks it to play. It also makes sure that we're looking in the correct folder for the music files.

Now that we have run through the key concepts of the Game Build, go to the *Get Coding!* website to download the complete code block for the side-scrolling platformer. You'll also find all the files you need to create the graphics and sounds. Look for the build tips if you get stuck or want to find out more about the concepts. Have fun!

Now go to the website and get coding your game!

WHAT NEXT?
YOUR GAMING FUTURE

Over the five missions in this book, you have not only helped the Lucky Cat Club win the Game On Hackathon but also learned some important new skills. You've coded a puzzle game, a game that ticks, and an endless runner. And finally, you've learned how to build a platform game with graphics, advanced collision detection, animations, enemies, and sound effects. Congratulations!

We hope that *Get Coding 2!* has shown you how fascinating building games can be. You've achieved a huge amount in each of the Game Builds. You also have some exciting challenges to take your Game Builds further. And there's still much more to learn!

When building your own games, don't be afraid to start off small. It's a better idea to begin with trying to code something achievable rather than building something that's so complicated you can't finish it. Don't expect your first game to look like the games you play for fun. And don't worry if you encounter bugs. Remember to access the developer tools in your browser to help you see where you might have gone wrong. This is a completely normal part of coding. No one gets it right the first time.

What will you code next?

Go to
www.getcodingkids.com
for more details

There are also some fantastic programs that you can build your games in that are more sophisticated than Notepad or TextEdit. These free tools make writing your code a little bit easier. The special text editors—sometimes called code editors or Integrated Development Environments (IDEs)—are used by developers all over the world. Try downloading Visual Studio Code for a helping hand. This program will color-code your code and automatically indent it, making it easier to key in and read.

There are also languages other than JavaScript that you can use to build games. Why not consider learning C++, Java, or C#? The syntax will be different, but the concepts will be similar. Give it a try!

Finally, remember that there are many other ways besides programming to be involved in building games. You could work on the graphics or on developing the storyline and characters for the game world. You could even compose the music and create the sound effects. The best games are built by teams of people who all contribute different skills.

The *Get Coding 2!* missions have been a great success. It's up to you what you do next.

INDEX

With thanks to my family and friends, who always get me through these Herculean endeavors. Thanks for the late nights, the burnout, and the support. Thank you to Rob Cooper for his technical review, and a thank-you to my friends at CG. And with infinite gratitude to my editor—without whose effort this couldn't happen. —D. W.

Text copyright © 2018 by David Whitney
Illustrations copyright © 2018 by Duncan Beedie

First U.S. edition 2019

Library of Congress Catalog Card Number pending
ISBN 978-1-5362-1030-9 (hardcover)
ISBN 978-1-5362-0541-1 (paperback)

19 20 21 22 23 24 LEO 10 9 8 7 6 5 4 3 2 1

Printed in Heshan, Guangdong, China

This book was typeset in Futura and Bokka.
The illustrations were created digitally.

Candlewick Press
99 Dover Street
Somerville, Massachusetts 02144

visit us at www.candlewick.com